CORPORATE UNDERTAKER

BUSINESS LESSONS FROM THE DEAD AND DYING

DOMENIC AVERSA

CONTENTS

INTRODUCTION

There are 28 million small businesses in America.
50% of them will fail in their first five years.
70% will fail in the first 10 years.

W hether you are self-employed or have a hundred employees, owning a business is difficult. Every day is filled with adversity. Either you get things right or you struggle to pay the bills. Sometimes, even when you get everything right, you still struggle to pay the bills.

From the moment you wake up there are challenges to overcome and there is a constant stream of worry and doubt. *Are my supplies getting delivered? Will they get the shipment correct? Are my customers going to make their appointments? Do I have enough money to buy new equipment? Is my website good enough? Did I log all of my accounting properly?* The list of questions never ends for a business owner, and the list usually grows longer throughout the day, every day.

Alongside the business concerns are your personal concerns. Very few people have the luxury of leaving their personal lives at the door. In most cases, your personal life gets woven into the business. Whether it's your health, your lifestyle, or your family, all of it comes to work with you.

Your spouse, kids, parents, in-laws, neighbors, friends, and all of the bills that surround your home all start to melt into one pile of never-ending responsibility. As an owner, an entrepreneur, and a leader, your job is to manage all of this every day. You have to keep everyone in your life—the entire extended sphere of your business and personal life—happy. You have to keep them employed, productive, and moving forward. Most of the time, you pull off this incredible act of strength and balance.

But then, one day, something slips through the cracks. Something doesn't get done. Something doesn't get paid. A vendor cuts off your credit. An important customer finds someone else. Something breaks. A key employee finds a new job. A family member is diagnosed with a terrible illness or something happens to you personally. You get sick, have an accident, or get divorced. Maybe you discover that you've been cheated, someone stole from you, lied to you, or stole from others.

Perhaps all of this happens at the same time. One challenge turns into another and then all of a sudden it is a pile of seemingly insurmountable problems. Adversity becomes crisis. You're out of time, you're out of money, you're overwhelmed, and you're not sure which way to turn.

Where do you go for help? There is no "oh shit" store. If you are religious, you can pray, and if you are spiritual, you can meditate. If you're neither, you can sit and stare into space. But then what? Who can help you through all of this? Who can help you avoid losing your business, losing your home, or losing your mind? Where do you turn? Can you turn to your lawyer, your accountant, or your best friend? They may be kind and they may be reliable, but none of them will have the right answers. They will give you the best answers from their own experiences. In general, they too have had several crises in their lives that they will relate to you for context. Even if they are good examples, you still have to get up every morning and work through what will now become an ever-growing list of adversity. Complaints will become lawsuits and lawsuits will require more energy, time, and money. The lawsuits become judgments and the judgments lead to bankruptcy. Years of striving and building are gone. Then more problems come. Where do you go from here? How do you pick up the pieces of your personal life? Regardless of what many would have you believe, business is personal.

The vast majority of small business owners never went to business school. They never studied accounting, marketing, or even social media. Most small business owners start a business in something they like or excel at. They cook, they weld, they clean; they are doctors, barbers, or bakers. They make, they sell. They are also very busy. Every day they have a long list of everything they need to be concerned with, and in general the least enjoyable part of their business is the *business* part. When times are good, they don't have to think about it so much. When times are bad, however, life becomes a miserable grind. The last thing they want to do is read a business book. Once in a while they come across very uplifting books that talk about concepts such as "The Seven Things," "The Five Things," or "The One Thing." They read the list, smile, and then compare it to their own list. Then they put the book down, thinking, "If life were only that easy."

Corporate Undertaker is not a book about easy things. It is about the countless personal and professional hardships that many of us in business face, day after day.

For more than 25 years I have been an entrepreneur and

crisis manager. In this period of time, I have covered a lot of ground. More than most business managers or owners will ever experience. I have travelled to 43 states in the US and done business with 60 different countries around the world. I worked with hundreds of small and mid-level sized companies as an operational manager, advisor, and investment banker. I have directly managed thousands of employees and advised on tens of thousands more. I have overseen the management of several billion in revenue and helped refinance an even greater amount of debt for struggling companies. Unfortunately, along this extensive journey, most of the time I was the last resort before these companies were liquidated.

The first question everyone asks me is, "What's the number one reason businesses fail?" My answer is always the same: a company never fails because of one mistake. A crisis in a company is not like a car accident; it doesn't just happen. It doesn't just show up out of nowhere and it's usually not one person's fault.

When a company is in deep trouble it's generally because they've made many mistakes over a long period of time and, usually, there is a group of people who have participated in its demise. In these situations, key managers and advisors have made bad decisions and then those bad decisions affect others outside of the company. Suppliers ship products even though they're having a tough time getting paid. Bankers renew credit lines despite the fact that they see declining metrics. Lawyers and accountants ease up on critical advice because they don't want to lose their client. Senior managers convince themselves that things will be better next quarter, mid-level managers stop complaining because they don't want to lose their jobs, and customers get frustrated but are happy to take discounts from a troubled company. All along the way, everyone is profiting in some manner. Improved margins, bonuses, benefits, job security—there's always some benefit to turning a blind eye to trouble.

Then one day, small problems become big problems, big problems spiral out of control, and everyone becomes fearful. That fear will manifest in different ways: greed, denial, panic, blame, anger, rage. All those people who cut corners, remained silent, and took bonuses are now responsible. They know it, but their insecurities and fears take over. They either grab what they can to solidify their position or they try to hide.

By the time I show up to a troubled company, the situation I find can be anything from a fever-pitched brawl over shrinking assets to a stale pile of waste that died a long time ago. Either I am thrown into a fire or I am corporate hospice. In either scenario, fear dominates. Everyone is upset, and they are trying to protect themselves. Everyone tied to the company has an opinion and has a competing interest. The owner, banker, suppliers, employees, and all of their respective lawyers are in a fight. It starts out quietly but then escalates as the company weakens. At the outset, they are arguing about money; they don't want to lose a penny. But in reality, they don't want to lose their jobs, their reputations, or their public standing. They screwed up and now they have to find a way out of this even if they have to lie, cheat, berate, cajole, manipulate, and abuse anyone and everyone, including me.

My job is to find an answer to all of their mistakes, fix the company, save jobs, get everyone back their money, and make sure that they don't kill each other—or me—in the process, and I have to do this before time runs out. The clock is ticking every hour of every day. A severely troubled company loses money every hour. At some point, time, credit, patience, and emotional stability will all run out. In short, my job is to buy time, find money, and create calm.

If I can't fix the company—if the mistakes are too great and the cash burn and debt burden are too far beyond reach—my job is to minimize the loss. In my world, this is the harsh reality; I am always called in too late.

I work in teams with very talented, hard-working, and conscientious professionals. They are experts in finance, operations, sales, law, and human psychology. We don't linger in conference rooms. We don't write fancy theoretical reports. We grind it out on the front lines with employees, suppliers, creditors, and customers, shoulder to shoulder, eyeball to eyeball. We work very fast, we rarely sleep, and we fight for every possible sign of survival. When you work with me, the message is clear: "never give up." However, despite our best efforts, 80% of our clients die. Consequently, while working in these dire conditions for many years, we've learned to make the absolute most out of the remains. If there is a flicker of light somewhere in the company, we will make it generate cash. In the end, the goal is to get as much money as possible paid back to suppliers and creditors to help preserve jobs at those companies.

Why do I do this work? Because I have lived through every stage of prosperity and adversity in a business myself. I do it because I know how hard it is to start and manage a business when it's successful and when, unfortunately, everything is going wrong. I do it because I want to help others in business avoid unnecessary suffering and unnecessary death.

I started in the business world as an optimistic, driven entrepreneur. I fought and educated myself out from a life of being poor and ignorant. Like many small business owners, my goal was simple: to be rich and free. But, like many, I soon discovered that all of the planning, faith, and optimism were no match for life. Despite my best efforts, I faced a never-ending stream of challenges, both personally and professionally. My journey in the business world became darker, uglier, and more complicated than I ever could have imagined or planned for. No business book ever prepared me for going to work with police escorts, firing thousands of people, and being witness to some of the worst behavior of the biggest banks and corporations in America. No MBA program could have prepared me for the physical and mental abuse on my body and being. It was a path filled with abuse of power, deceit, corruption, and death threats, all in the name of business. After years of fighting for life— the life of a business and the lives of employees—I changed in every way possible. I was no longer a businessman; I was an advocate.

In this book, I am going to take you on a journey that spans the first 25 years of my life in business. It reads like a highly charged, dramatic, and compelling entrepreneurial thriller. It's a race to the sun. Toward the fire. At times it is graceful but mostly it's exhausting, frustrating, and ugly. However, despite this unrelenting terrain, I endured and I survived. I took a lot of abuse and I often lost but I never stopped. I picked myself up each time and went on to the next fight. I didn't ask to be a hero but I felt a tremendous amount of responsibility to never stop looking for solutions. I would rather die than give up searching and exploring ways to save jobs, companies—lives, including my own.

What did I bring back with me from this long, winding, and grueling trip? Knowledge and wisdom. Lessons for an entire lifetime in business. I am a virtual library of commerce for all things bad and destructive. I am also a reservoir of creativity, dreams, and inspiration. To survive any journey you need to understand all of the dangers in the road, but you also have to maintain a strong sense of optimism. There is a lot that I learned from the dead and dying—and, now I want to share it with you.

I will take you through the timeline continuum of critical points in business: life, adversity, crisis, death, and rebirth. I will share with you my life experience in becoming an entrepreneur as well as stories from my work as a crisis manager. It is anything but the typical path in the corporate world.

I'm going to share with you stories of chaos, confusion, desperation, and loss. Some are extremely violent and menacing. However, I will also include stories of hope, reinvention, and regrowth. It will be the complete path of what many of us experience in our own lives.

Through each stage, I will give you lessons and tools that help you with crisis: either avoiding it, managing through it, or recovering from it. In the end, I hope to give you skills and tools to avoid unnecessary suffering and unnecessary death.

The biggest lesson I have learned from the dead and dying: be brave in the face of adversity. When you are brave, you have taken the first step toward joy—you are telling the world, "I may lose this fight but you're going to see the best of me."

Now, take a deep breath and let's begin this walk through my corporate cemetery.

PREFACE

I wasn't sure who I was or what I had become.
I was tired.
I was in pain.
Those were the only two certainties in my life at age 45.

I wasn't in a combat sport, but it certainly felt like it. The sheer intensity of my work and lifestyle had taken a brutal toll on me.

Two molars had just been pulled from my mouth. My dentist wondered openly why I had so much stress in my life. Like others, he tried to counsel me on how to relax. And, like others, he was just an apparition to me. I could barely hear what he was saying. We then discussed treating the other four teeth I had apparently crushed from the constant gnawing and grinding.

Each night, the strain of looking at thousands of numbers throughout the day stressed the muscles around my eyes to the point where they were swollen. On most days, it felt as if someone had been repeatedly punching me in the head. I routinely packed a bag with ice and covered my face with it just to stop the throbbing.

I barely slept but when I did manage to sleep, I slept on

the floor. Initially, I would try to sleep on a bed however, after 15 minutes of lying on the bed, a searing hot bolt of pain would shoot through my lower back. I knew it was coming each time, but I still wanted 15 minutes on a bed so I could feel some semblance of not being lost and homeless. If I stayed one minute longer, the pain would shoot up to my head. Frustrated and not wanting any more shock therapy, I'd gather the sheets and spread them out on the floor and pass out. I would wake up, usually four or five hours later, in the middle of the night; the first thing I did was smell my hands. I was exhausted and disoriented. The smell of soap on my hands would tell me what hotel I was in. I travelled so much, I would often forget where I was. In the dark, on a cold cement floor, the scent of soap was the only reliable compass: floral=Westin, pine=Marriott, slight musk=Hilton. Today, it was Hilton.

Once a week, in search of more energy, I would visit a naturopathic doctor, implausibly named Dr. Nirvana. She was petite, stunning, and eternally blissful. Every week she would give me an intravenous injection filled with a cocktail of vitamins, and every week she would look at me quizzically and ask, "Why do you work so hard? I don't understand why anyone would want to do your job. Do you not like yourself?"

I actually wasn't sure of the answer. I knew that I used to like myself. I used to like a lot of things, but now I wasn't sure. I was in the 15th month of an assignment that was only supposed to have lasted six months. This project was on the West Coast and I lived on the East Coast. I was too tired from work and flying to other cities to make the flight home every weekend, so, often, I just stayed at the hotel. After more than eight months of doing this, I decided to move out of my apartment in New York City. I put everything into storage and made the hotel my official address. At the same time, I decided to leave my consulting firm. I gave up my partnership and was now employed as an independent contractor. I made up my mind that I was done with the business world. This would be my last client. I would finish up here and then I would go somewhere else. I wasn't sure where, but I knew it would be somewhere far away from human beings. I had spent decades learning to salvage and repair many things. I knew very well that there were limits to everything, including time, energy, and emotions. I also knew that things break, including people and souls, and I knew that I was broken—probably for longer than I cared to admit.

But at this moment, none of that mattered—I still had responsibilities. As a consultant, a little more than a year earlier, I was appointed interim COO of this client's company, a struggling, $135M multi-national apparel manufacturer. I knew that I had to finish turning this company around. I knew that if I failed, this company would eventually fall, and with it, a cascade of people would be affected. Four hundred employees within the actual company could lose their jobs. Suppliers that didn't get paid by us would certainly have to fire some of their own employees. The bank that extended $30 million of credit would also incur a loss. So, at this moment in time, my pain and fatigue were irrelevant when I thought about all of those people and their families. It was my job to never lose hope, to always find a way out of trouble, and to bring clarity and certainty, regardless of the level of crisis.

When my partner and I first started at the company, it was burning more than a million a month in cash. Now, it was break-even. By most standards it was a successful turnaround, but by my standards it still needed to improve or it would eventually be back in financial trouble. It still did not have all of the proper pieces or strategy in place. We knew what needed to be put in place to ensure its future success, but our client, the owner, refused to make those final, important changes. Despite more than a year of kindly, cautiously, respectfully, and even rudely telling him that he was the biggest problem with the business, he refused to change his managerial style or his views on strategy.

The owner saw himself as prodigy of business, so he dragged out decision-making on all of our plans. He dug in his heels, complained, winced, pounded the table, yelled, and even shed tears whenever we suggested major changes to his company. He claimed that he had a vision of greatness and world domination that needed to happen. He had been a great success. He had multiple homes and boats and his face had graced the cover of magazines. He had built a library for his accomplishments in apparel. He firmly believed that he was a genius in the design of clothing. He also saw himself as a revolutionary. He planted trees for the community and gave eloquent speeches on conservation and saving the planet. He was certain that he was right. He was a dragon slayer. A mythical god in the making. In his mind he was all of these things; however, he just couldn't accept the fact that his company had lost more than 40% market share and had not made a profit in more than four years. He also seemed oblivious to the fact that he had personally lost more than $30M in the past six years financing the losses of this company. In his mind, he was always right. Gods never make mistakes. And to prove it, he had three public relations firms on retainer telling the world that he was a genius, so how could he be wrong? When he finally did concede to a change, it was because he had rationalized a way to blame someone else for the shortcoming.

When we started on this project, we found countless "yes" men and women at the company. In one of the operational files, there was a memo from the previous COO that read, "The CEO doesn't like to hear the word 'no'. He also doesn't like confrontation. So, please avoid these two things with him at all costs." It was an absolute Never Never Land, staffed with Peter Pan and the Lost Boys and Girls.

Dozens of employees were on the payroll who didn't actually do any constructive work. They were busy but they weren't helpful to the company. They surfed, got high, and hung out. Many of their bosses weren't much better. Some meant well but they too were misfits and curious wanderers. There were a lot of people filling desks and offices but nothing ever seemed to change or improve. They tried but they had little guidance from above. Most of the executive management had no formal business education or outside managerial experience. They had risen through the ranks, with many starting in sales or the warehouse. Some worked hard, but much of the management style was ad hoc and from "the gut." However, even when someone had good experience and skills, they weren't able to do their jobs effectively because of the obstacles put in front of them by the owner. It was a company filled with indifference and denial.

The owner refused to show anyone complete financial statements; instead, he showed them sales and gross margins. He never revealed the true picture. People knew that sales were sliding but as far as they knew, the company was profitable. In a desperate attempt to keep up appearances, the owner paid out $800k in bonuses a month before we started. No one knew of the actual debt levels, burning cash, and mounting losses.

Additionally, despite failing for several years, no one ever got fired. Peter Pan had never fired one person in his entire business career. Why should he? Life in Never Never Land was fun. Rooms were filled with ping-pong tables and pinball games, there were constant parties all around the world, and there even was an entire building with a skateboard park. While everyone was having fun, product quality dropped, on-time deliveries suffered, margins evaporated, cash burned, and competition rose quickly.

As the company got smaller, budgets shrank. Salespeople only knew how to have fun; they were not held responsible for contribution margins or net margins, so they sold products at a loss. Product lines lost their edge and became stale in the marketplace. The cool people and cool stores waned on these tired designs. By the time we got there, seven of the top 10 customers were discount retailers. They had a young customer base but little investment in modern technology. They had virtually no sales by ecommerce; they didn't understand it. The list of weaknesses was never-ending.

It seemed as though every single department needed to be fixed, from merchandising to logistics, finance to sales. But the biggest and most menacing problem was with their strategy. They had five brands that were all competing for the same customer. They thought that they had five strategies, but they barely had one. Finally, there were legal issues, which was not surprising, since the Lost Boys and Girls had been sloppy in all of their business dealings. There were stacks of litigation against them that had piled up from around the world with potential damages amounting to tens of millions. Despite all of these issues and despite the chaos and obvious crisis, we still felt like we could save this company. We just had to get the owner to agree with changing the things that had gotten them into trouble.

In situations like these, generally, you start with the big issues, change the strategy, and then align the operation from there. But in this case, we had to do the opposite. The owner refused to make any major significant strategic changes. We could make minor changes but not the big ones that would actually have a long-term benefit. Being Peter Pan, he viewed his brands as his "babies." When I suggested getting rid of several brands, quizzically and with grand indignation, he asked, "Would you kill your baby?" Plainly, I stared at him and answered, "If my baby was losing millions of dollars each year, I would. And if, for some reason, I couldn't kill it, I would give it up for adoption." He laughed and said, "You're so funny." He never could comprehend that I wasn't trying to be funny.

Typically, when you have conversations like this, a rational person would leave the engagement. Just shut down your laptop and leave. An experienced crisis manager knows that a person like this owner is delusional, controlling, and destructive. We've seen enough in the crisis world to know that this is not going to end well. We should have quit right at the beginning when we knew he wouldn't commit to the bigger changes. But we didn't; we stayed. It's our job to stay. It's our job to work around and beyond the ignorance and obstruction of owners and leaders of troubled companies. That's what we do. We're generally the last option before a company shuts down. If the company shuts down, hundreds of people are hurt, so despite having to deal with this massive narcissist, we kept moving forward. If we left a job every time we faced an impossible situation, we'd never have work.

So, without the ability to actually make big strategic decisions, we devised a plan to fix everything internally and buy time. We figured that we could cut losses dramatically and perhaps earn the owner's trust so that he'd eventually let us make the bigger changes.

The owner reluctantly agreed to the plan and then proceeded to challenge it every step of the way. Why? Because it wasn't his plan. He wanted the company to improve, but if WE fixed it, it meant that HE had actually done things wrong in the past. Peter Pan was never wrong. So, he insisted on hearing about every decision that we made and every direction we gave to every manager throughout the entire company. He would bellyache and annoy us incessantly. He sent a steady stream of emails to us. There were emails first thing in the morning, emails throughout the day, and emails in the evening and on weekends. At one point through the course of the year, my mother became severely ill, contracted sepsis, and had to be put in a medically induced coma. Upon hearing this news, I immediately flew to my parents' hometown in the Midwest. I told the owner that I needed to be with my mother and father because she was in intensive care and the doctors were uncertain if she would survive this infection. How did he respond? "Okay, but when will you be back? The company needs you." I said nothing.

I was gone two weeks. While I sat with my mother, as she lay in a coma, in intensive care, Peter Pan sent me no less than 10 emails a day, every day, asking for updates on different areas of the company. It was a very conflicting, frustrating time. Every day, I prayed to God to save my mother. And every day, I prayed to the same God to take my life or the life of my man-child client. God is far nicer than I could ever be. He spared all of us. Thankfully, my mother survived. I, however, would have to return to the certain virtual death of dealing with the megalomaniacal narcissist of the clothing world.

The obsessive controlling didn't end at emails. There were also, in person, three-hour "update" meetings twice per week. Over and over and over he would ask, "What is happening?" Line by line, we would tell him and then he would question every decision. He was constantly asking, "Are you sure? Are you sure?" He'd leave our meetings and go tell others what we were thinking of doing; then he'd come back and tell us that everyone disagreed. He kept soliciting advice from the very people who had driven the company into failure. When we tried to fire someone, he insisted on having a discussion with that person about how they might feel if they were to be fired. People became angry and frustrated and worked even less. For months, we couldn't fire anyone. Three months passed, and all we were doing was rearranging departments and desks. It took us four months to convince him to show managers the contribution and net margins for the products they were making and selling. It took us six months before we could dismantle the skateboard park and sell the building it was in to generate cash to operate the business. And it was nine months before we could talk him into getting rid of non-profitable customers. Overall, it was sheer and utter madness encased in a slow, melting grind.

As crisis managers, we are hired because of our ability to move quickly; but there we were, stuck in a swamp of vanity and ineptness. Yet, out of loyalty and a sense of responsibility to the firm, friends, countless creditors, and hundreds of employees, we stayed.

Despite the obstacles and resistance, as the months continued to pass, we muscled through, dragging and persuading him and others to come along with the changes. We fired weak employees and replaced them with truly talented people. We found many bright spots within the company and gave promotions to those who had been outshined by "yes" men and women. Product quality improved dramatically. On-time shipping was nearly perfect, margins improved on every item, product offering narrowed and sharpened, and e-commerce was put into high gear. We shed useless customers and weak salespeople and settled countless outstanding litigation. Millions in losses were now nonexistent. The company was out of crisis and close to returning to a path of success. The company still had to improve its long-term strategic direction, but for now, it was relatively stable.

It was legitimately satisfying to have made these significant improvements after the long slog. And, it was fun when we actually found light underneath the piles of bad managers. It was now exciting to finally be working with a talented, conscientious, and kind group of people around the world. But, it was as if it all happened too late. Now, seemingly at the end of the climb, at the part when you're on top and get to enjoy the view, I couldn't. I was worn out and in pain. Not just from this client but from all of my clients. I was worn out by more than 20 years of living through perpetual crises. Years of nonstop arguing and fighting and countless hours of absorbing fear and anger. I became even more weary when I tried to figure why I had done all of this. Why had I chosen this path? Why did I try so hard? Wasn't there an easier way?

Then, one day, Dr. Nirvana called me to review my most

recent bloodwork. She was not her normal spritely and optimistic self. Apparently, my lab results looked very bad—worse than usual. My blood pressure was sky high and my cholesterol and glucose were even higher. My hormone levels were all wrong and my kidneys were failing. Worst of all was my liver; the liver enzymes were 17 times what they are supposed to be. She consulted with three other doctors and they all agreed that I should be admitted to a hospital immediately.

I'm a crisis manager for a living, so I don't panic in a crisis. This was a crisis—MY crisis—but it wasn't my first. This just seemed like another day in my life. It wasn't the news I had hoped for, but I wasn't alarmed. I simply said, "Okay, thank you. I'm okay. I'll be fine once I stop working. I'm not going to go to the hospital. I just need a little sleep."

It seems ridiculous, but in my mind my health didn't matter. Quite frankly, I was surprised that I had lived that long. I never thought I would reach the age of 45. For the past 20 years my death always seemed to be looming. Despite all of this lousy news, my only thought was to continue working. I put my health concerns aside and carried on.

We couldn't fix the strategy because of the owner, so the last big piece was to refinance the senior debt. The existing bank wanted out of the loan much earlier in the engagement but it wasn't possible because of the previous cash burn. However, now that the company improved and seemed to be on stable ground, obtaining a new lender was very achievable. If I could finish this one last thing, I would have a sense of completion of a job well done and then I could fade into the sunset. I could retire from this work and this project knowing that we did everything possible to save this company. Once the refinancing was complete, the burden of the long-term strategies was up to the owner. I just needed to hang on for another three or four months.

The owner hired his own investment bankers without consulting me or my team. That action alone was very suspicious. The so-called "legitimate" investment bankers took on a client without looking at financial statements from the CFO or operational statements from the COO. Then, the owner, with his personal financial advisor, decided to also hire a new attorney for the company—again, without consulting with us. Together, in the coming weeks, this new team of mysterious characters put together a refinance prospectus. Throughout the process, we provided them with as much comprehensive detail and support as was available.

As a matter of practice, everyone who goes through a process like this generally shows optimistic projections. But in this instance, they were beyond optimism. They took the numbers we had given them and inflated them beyond recognition. They showed current projections that exceeded the amount of inventory we had or could buy. It was physically impossible to sell product that we didn't have or could have made. Therefore, their numbers were fictional; also known as *fraud*.

Round and round we went debating the legitimacy of their projections. They needed the COO and CFO to sign off on these numbers to have credibility in the marketplace, but we refused. There was no way we were going to send out numbers to the finance community that were knowingly false and designed to induce a transaction. It was then I realized that they had a separate quest. They were not just trying to refinance the company; they were looking for potential buyers or investors. They had convinced themselves that the company was worth $300M. Therefore, they needed numbers that would substantiate that claim. In my experience, unless there was a significant change in strategy, the company was worth no more than $75M. Unquestionably, there was a big disparity. I was willing to construct a legitimate plan that demonstrated continued change, but I was not willing to commit fraud. To the new deal team, it wasn't a crime; it was just hopeful projections. Their rationalization was that everyone knows projections aren't accurate. To me it was nonsensical bullshit.

We went on like this for a couple weeks. I tried to persuade them to change their position and then, finally, out of desperation, I asked the owner to fire me. I just couldn't do it any longer. But, at the same time, I couldn't quit either. Which was ridiculous. In the past, in the face of a crime, I would walk out in an instant. I don't know what happened to me. I'm not sure if it was just utter fatigue, confusion, or pain, but, either way, I felt stuck. I wanted things to be proper and right but I was out of steam to make anything happen.

Then one day, the owner scheduled a 7 a.m. conference call that included his personal financial advisor, his lawyer, the CFO, and me. Within seconds of joining the call, he began to read a prepared letter. I had asked him to fire me so, now, he honored my request. By 7:01 a.m. I was terminated. I was booted out of Never Never Land.

I was upset that they had chosen to remove me instead of using proper projections. However, I was strangely happy. My career as a crisis manager was finally over. I could be free of all of this consternation. Within 10 minutes, however, the ugliness of working in a troubled environment with highly dysfunctional people would come back to haunt me.

I tried to email a few managers to let them know what had happened, but my email account was locked, so I texted a few people but received no response. Within minutes I received a text from the owner's lawyer threatening to sue me if I contacted any employees, suppliers, or customers. Hours passed, and I heard from only a couple people. Brief messages of shock and wishing me well. However, it was strangely silent.

One manager did eventually connect with me. He called me and told me that the owner and his team gave explicit instructions to all employees that no one was to contact me in any manner. The implied message was *"If you do, you're the next one to be fired."* So, they managed to silence the entire staff with fear.

Then, before the end of the day, a courier arrived at the door with a formal cease and desist letter in which they threatened to sue me for all damages that might arise if a refinancing or divesture did not happen. It was swift and well planned—*shut him up, put him in a box, and threaten to take everything from him.* It was very persuasive but it wasn't enough for Pan and his team. They went one step further. *Discredit him.*

Within a couple of days, word came back to me that the owner had told everyone he fired me because I was trying to devalue the company so that I could buy it on the cheap. He claimed that I was trying to steal the company from him and that when I did, many people would lose their jobs. He, his lawyer, his personal financial advisor, and his investment bankers told this story over and over to as many as they could; to the majority of employees, the managers, friends, bankers, and everyone on their refinance list, private equity firms and their lawyers. They kept me locked out and gagged with threats of lawsuits, so they could spin their story. All of this for what? So that they could shop around their fictitious financial projections, artificially pump up the value of the company, make the owner wealthier, and get more money for everyone involved. Bigger fees, bigger bonuses, and even bigger egos by bragging about the giant deal they were brokering. Of course, it didn't matter if it was a lie. It didn't matter that it all could fall apart in less than a year when the projections didn't manifest. It just mattered that anyone who didn't go along with the plan was removed from the process so a deal could be closed.

I had spent more than a year giving everything I had trying to save this company. I worked 80-hour weeks. I lived in a hotel. I sacrificed my body, my relationship with my family, and my friends. I put up with an endless barrage of insults, threats, ineptitude, and manipulation. Through all of this, with my team, we succeeded in turning the company around, saving hundreds of jobs and millions of dollars, and what did I get for it? Ousted and sullied. Just another shining example of a spoiled and privileged country club from a group of businessmen and women who saw me as a threat because I wouldn't go along with their deception. Welcome to the world of business.

A year earlier, everyone was ready to march this company into bankruptcy court; it was busted and broke and no one saw the light of day. But now that it was shiny and new, greed would prevail. After a year of injecting good will and good process into this company it didn't matter. In the end it was all thrown out in exchange for dirty money.

I started my life in business in a cataclysmic trial by fire. And now, two decades later, it was just as it began; surrounded by liars, cheats, and thieves. They had won. I was beaten, disheartened, and broken.

I know that I chose this life. I chose the most difficult and oftentimes riskiest environments to work in, but something in me hoped for more. Hoped for better. At a minimum, some decency. However, it never came. Once again, I had been betrayed. I couldn't take any more of it. I was empty. I had spent my entire business life living amongst the dead and dying, and now I had become one of them.

I was done. I couldn't live one more day in this perpetual world of corporate death and destruction. This was my last client. I called the colleagues on my team and told them that I was going to disappear for a very long time. They asked, "Where are you going?"

I said, "I don't know. I think I'm just going to go lay down in the sand by the ocean or maybe in a wheat field on a giant, tranquil farm. I just need to sleep because right now, I'm not sure if I'm dead or alive." I hung up and went to bed. I just needed to think about how I actually had gotten here.

LIFE

What makes a person start a business? What makes a person want to manage or lead a business? Is it circumstance or by design? Do we do it for love or money? Why would someone want this extra responsibility?

There are as many different answers as there are people. Some are pursuing a passion. Some are pursuing wealth. Others want freedom. Most just want to be the boss.

Whatever the reason, I believe that most business owners and managers never really know how much is involved in keeping a business afloat and steady through a storm. If they did, they would be doing something else.

I know for me, that certainly was what happened through my business life. I could have never imagined the improbable path that I would take simply because I wanted to make money.

I always thought that my life would go up and up; that it would follow a logical progression of success. It didn't seem like a big stretch. Parents, teachers, and all of the advertising in the world said, "If you study hard and work hard then life will reward you." To a certain extent, up until the age of 23, this had been true for me.

It was a very proud day when I got accepted into law

1

school. It had been a long journey; not only for me, but for my entire family. For both my father and my mother, education meant everything. All of my grandparents had only finished third grade. My father had only an eighth-grade education and, my mother had dropped out of high school to get married. Now, being the first person on both sides of the family to go to law school was an incredible achievement for all of us. The family was advancing. We had moved out of the fields and factories and into the halls of power and adjudication.

Most of my family were farmers in Central Italy. Mostly with grain but they were surrounded by the usual suspects found in barns: chickens, sheep, pigs, and cows. Post-WWII, after facing many years of austerity, they went seeking a better life. They moved to Southern Ontario, Canada, and took jobs in the auto factories and construction industry. It was a family of workers. They believed in working hard and being productive. There was no such thing as "just hanging out." From morning to night, you either had to be at a job or at school. It was a strong work ethic that was borne out of hunger, war, and loss. It was a belief that you had an obligation to yourself and the entire extended family to work and study hard. This was an environment where we were constantly learning. When I wasn't in school, I could be helping my father and grandfather mix cement, build a wall or a sidewalk, put shingles on a roof, change brakes on a car, landscape the yard. Or, I could be helping my mother make pasta and bread each week, pick and can tomatoes, peppers, pickles, peaches…and, essentially anything that could be grown and preserved. From the age of eight, I was helping to make wine and prosciutto. By the time I was 14, I was studying algebra at school and then learning to measure with a string line. I could calculate the angles and grade of a new driveway or new sod in a yard with either my calculator or 50 feet of twine. It was a wonderful balance between reading books and learning to work with my hands.

We were no longer farmers but we still lived close to the earth. I learned how to grow, how to salvage, and also how to kill. From my earliest memories, I was taught the entire circle of life. It began by starting at the very end of another life – by shoveling manure; anything from pigs, sheep, or horse. Each had a distinct effect on what was needed for our soil and garden. If you want good tomatoes and zucchini, you better know what your sheep had for lunch.

I shoveled, turned soil, planted, watered, weeded, and waited for nature to produce something all of us could eat. Most kids played baseball and soccer in the summer; I played farmer. And, when I wasn't gardening, I was helping my parents butcher an animal. Today, for most, this sounds like a brutal and foreign phenomena. However, for me and my family, it was just what we did for food. Chickens, rabbits, goats, pigs, cows, fish, and even, once, a moose were slaughtered, gutted, and butchered at our home. It was messy, smelly, and sometimes repugnant, but it was food. It was life. It's what we did to survive and get by with little money.

We weren't statistically poor but we certainly didn't have much to spare. I learned not to waste anything. Old nails were straightened out. Branches from a willow tree were used to bind wood. There was no such thing as "scrap." We were always told "it may be useful someday." Everything from food to clothing was shared with the extended family as well as neighbors. Every August there was a procession of boxes filled with children's clothes. Before school started,

3

our moms would pass the older kids' clothes to the younger kids. I wore most of my cousin's clothes until I was 14. At the time, it didn't really bother me that they weren't from a store; they were still new to me.

My family arrived in Canada with not more than a couple of suitcases, but their work ethic kept us all moving forward and upward, one step at a time. We spent the first five years of my life living with my grandparents. Then my parents bought their own house. By the time I was 10, we were able to buy a new car for the first time, right off the dealership lot. By age 11, we got a dryer for our clothes. At 12, central air-conditioning. At 14, I was allowed to buy new clothes for school. In my mind, this was living the high life. The formula worked. Stick together, help each other, and keep at it. And, that's exactly what I did all the way until I reached the crowning moment: law school.

I received praise and accolades far and wide. The well-wishes extended through many neighborhoods and as far back as Italy. My parents, grandparents, uncles, and aunts all had the same feeling—"we've arrived."

There was only one problem: I now hated the notion of practicing law. It had been a long journey, but it was ruined for me the first day of orientation week.

I sat in the auditorium with 144 classmates, eagerly awaiting an inspirational speech from one of the most successful attorneys in the city. This portly, well-suited man stood in front of the class, and his first words were, "The law is a jealous mistress." *A what? A who? Mistress? What the hell is he talking about? I think he meant minstrel. A poet, a singer. It had to be a minstrel.*

He continued. "She will always call you back. She won't let you leave her side. You will abandon family and friends

4

for her. She will seduce you to a point of insanity. But, in the end, you will be a better lawyer for her."

Yeah, he meant mistress.

Shit.

Unbelievable. I had worked tirelessly for years to try to get to this place. Days, weeks, months, YEARS stuck in a library, morning to night. For this? To work at something where I would alienate friends and family—for what? A big bag of gold for a girlfriend?

What a disappointment.

From that moment on, I pretty much mentally checked out. I would still go to classes because I loved studying law, but the more I learned about the realities of practicing law the more I hated it. It was a life consumed with splitting words and phrases and billing as many hours as you possibly could before you died. I knew that there had to be more to life than being chained to a desk, sifting through piles of legal briefs, carefully logging my billable hours in increments of 10 minutes, constantly looking for colorful ways to tell clients I am adding value and worth every penny I charge them. There had to be a better option.

Then one day, before the end of my first year of law school, a brand-new opportunity presented itself. I came across a flyer on a bulletin board advertising a program studying the implications of having a common European Market (the EU) that would go into effect in 1992. It was a joint program between the University of Manchester, England and the Moscow Institute of International Affairs, Soviet Union. I knew nothing about any of these places or about any common business market, but I figured that it was really far away and that it was really different than law, so I would try it.

Without much planning or fanfare, in the summer of 1991, I found myself in Moscow, USSR. The Soviet Union was both fascinating and disturbing. It was fascinating because I actually felt like I was behind a curtain, probably more of a cement one than iron. No matter where you turned, the city felt distant and closed off. Prior to this trip, I knew nothing about Russians or communism. What little I knew came from watching movies like *Top Gun* and *Rocky IV*. I also knew that the Russians were our "mortal enemies." The Great Soviet Union was a leader in all things: space exploration, athletics, medicine, science, engineering, and, of course, chess and ballet. They were the other superpower; the counterbalance to America.

I'm not sure what I expected to see when I arrived in Moscow, but I should have had a clue while I was in Manchester. Before we left England, the Russian students filled multiple suitcases with toiletries such as toothpaste, soap, shampoo, lotions, and creams; ordinary and basic items that we can find at any pharmacy or grocery store in the United States. I found it a bit odd, but I just thought they just wanted different products—things they couldn't find in their country. However, now that I was actually in Moscow, I realized that they couldn't find *any* products. None. The few stores that I did come across were barren. It wasn't only the stores, however; the entire city seemed like a ghost town. There were people and many buildings, but everyone and everything seemed to be shadows of themselves. There was only a whiff of spirit and soul. There was little color and no advertising or neon signs. In every direction there were endless rows of large, cement buildings.

As I walked around, I noticed that the city was spotless. Then it dawned on me that it was so clean because there was nothing to throw away. There were no bags, paper cups, or candy bar wrappers. I walked past an open plaza. I saw 30 people lined up in front of a vending machine. As I got closer, I stopped to watch a very unusual process. When people reached the vending machine, they put in a coin and pressed a button, and water would come down into a five-ounce glass. They would swirl the water around and then throw it out. They'd place the glass back down and press another button, and the glass would be filled with Pepsi. They drank their soda and left the glass for the next person. They were so poor that there was a shortage on materials like tin and glass. I just stared and wondered, *This is a superpower?" We were afraid of these guys?* Later I would come to understand that there was good reason to fear them; they spent 35% of their GDP on military expenditures.

Meanwhile, the citizens walked around with "just in case" bags. There were so few products in the stores that they bartered for anything they needed. To accommodate a possible purchase, they always carried a bag "just in case" they found something to buy or trade.

My school program was being offered by one of Moscow's top academic institutions. MGIMO, as it was known, was reserved for the best and brightest of high-ranking Soviet Party members. As such, we were treated very well. Each night, we were offered their very best in dining and entertainment. Their music showed signs of life from their rich and dramatic history. Unfortunately, however, their food options couldn't hide the ugly reality of the poverty running through the country. Each meal generally consisted of butter, pumpernickel bread, and a small piece of tough and fatty beef. That was their best, so I was grateful. Fortunately, there seemed to be no shortage of caviar and vodka. I had never tried caviar prior to this trip, so I wouldn't know how to distinguish good from bad. I only knew that it was some semblance of food and that there were three-pound tins on every table.

Our accommodations were as drab and desolate as the rest of the city. My room had the added benefit of being absolutely infested with cockroaches. There were so many roaches that they were pouring out of the sink and bathtub drains. I could not turn on the water without having dozens of cockroaches come pouring out. It was a disgusting stream of black, shiny, creepy-crawly things racing to save their lives. It was intolerable. However, in a desperate attempt to have some semblance of peace when I slept, I bought several bottles of vodka to use as a disinfectant. The vodka smelled and tasted like pure rubbing alcohol. I would periodically wipe down all of the walls and floors just to keep them off of me and my clothes.

Most nights, to avoid going back to my room, I would stay at the restaurant. One night, after having drunk a little too much, I found myself on the subway with a couple of my classmates. They were from South Carolina and they loved Jimmy Buffet. Being young and happy, we were having a good time singing "Margaritaville" on the train ride back to our dormitory. I hadn't noticed those standing around me or others seated, but they certainly were paying attention to us. Unannounced, an old man in a ragged gray coat rose from his seat and lunged at me with a long knife. I didn't see him until he was a couple of inches from my chest. Fortunately for me, one of my new friends was an ex-Marine. He saw the old man and pulled me out of the way at the last minute.

The old man sat back down, grumbling something in Russian. I looked at him and said, "I'm sorry." He had tried to stab me in the chest with a five-inch knife, but somehow I felt like I had it coming to me. I felt bad for him. I could sense that there was some greatness that had once existed in Russia but now it was gone and now there were talks about another revolution and taking down all remnants of the Soviet Empire. A cultural, political, and economic change was coming that seemed very promising to many people. But to others, like this older gentleman, it meant erasing everything he had ever known. He and others like him thought, *You told us we were the greatest. Why now do we have to change?* Now, in front of him, instead of a quiet ride home on a subway, he had to listen to young idiots singing songs he didn't know. If I were him, I might have wanted to stab me, too.

The program ended, and I left Moscow not really knowing what to make of it. A few weeks later a first coup attempt was launched against the government. Boris Yeltsin sent tanks into Red Square. By the end of the year, the Soviet Union was dissolved, and it was replaced with a democratic and capitalistic model of government under the name Commonwealth of Independent States (CIS).

Soon thereafter, I was back in Canada when I received a telephone call from one of my Russian classmates. He asked me if I would help him start a business. He really didn't know what type of business to start; he just knew that he wanted to be a "capitalist."

He presented me with a wide range of options: aluminum, oil, cars, furs, and bee pollen. It was very exciting because it didn't seem like there was a limit to the possibilities. Russia, in particular, was barren. They needed every possible consumer item for the home, but they also needed to rebuild their infrastructure. They needed electricity, roads, garbage removal, and gas stations. After a long and positive conversation, I ended by telling him, "This is all great. I just need to think about a few things."

The reality is that I didn't know anything about business. I didn't even know where to start. As much as I didn't like the idea of practicing law, in my mind, it was guaranteed employment. This opportunity with the Russians sounded interesting, but who knew where it would lead? It could be a big waste of time.

I was back in school, but still debating this opportunity, when I read an article in the local paper that said that the first Italian Canadian had been appointed to the Supreme Court of Canada. As an Italian, I found this exciting. My family and friends had dinner parties all of the time, so I thought, *Let's have one for the judge.* Not knowing any better or thinking twice about it, I immediately wrote him a letter and invited him to our city for a dinner. Within two weeks I got a letter from him saying, "Thank you for the kind words and the invitation, but I will be unable to attend a dinner." I was amused but also annoyed, thinking, *Who doesn't want a dinner party in their honor?* I then went to the dean of the university, a former dean of the Faculty of Law and a fellow Italian. I told him my thoughts. He liked the idea and immediately said, "I know Frank. I'll call him." I thought "Wow. He calls him by his first name. Cool." I said, "Thank you," and left his office. Two days later the dean called me at home and said, "Okay, kid, he's coming in six weeks. He'll be here for three days. Make the arrangements and tell me where I need to be." And then he hung up.

I was smiling but I was very confused. I had requested *a dinner,* not a three-day visit, and I didn't say that I would organize it. I thought it was a good idea, but I thought someone else would do it. Someone with more experience in these matters. What did I know about planning a dinner party like this? I only knew how to show up and eat, and now I had to figure out what to do with him for three days. What do you do with a Supreme Court judge for three days? I didn't have a clue. But fortunately, I was Italian, and I had a big family. Someone would have the answers.

I had an uncle who ran an Italian dinner and cultural club. He routinely hosted parties for more than a thousand people, so he walked me through the entire punch list of tasks. He prepared an extensive menu from the judge's home province in Italy, so that part was done. Next, I had to make sure that a lot of people came to the dinner. I had a cousin who was president of the Italian Business Association. I went to him and asked for help and he moved their monthly meeting to the same night as this dinner. With this move, I instantly had a few hundred people in attendance—all prominent professionals and businessmen in the community. I then needed to further elevate the dinner environment so proceeded to call every politician I could across the region—federal, provincial, and local. I offered them free tickets and the seat location of their choice. Everyone accepted. Politicians never miss an opportunity to raise funds and smile for the camera.

With dinner taken care of, I quickly filled in the other time slots. It was easier than I thought; they came to me. Everyone wanted to be close to the justice. The Canadian ambassador to Italy wanted to host a party, and so did the dean of the university and the Law Society and Student Council. The agenda was complete. I could now exhale.

A couple of weeks later, I picked him up at the airport. I met a very humble, generous, and astutely intelligent man named Justice Frank Iacobucci. I spent three days chauffeuring and escorting him to speaking engagements and dinner parties. It was grand. People fawned and showered him with praise. Rooms filled with well-heeled and well-connected folks. Everyone ate from small plates but drank from large glasses. They were elegant and confident and looked to be enjoying life. The closer I stood to the justice, the greater the respect I was shown. All of a sudden, I am no longer a lowly, broke student. I'm in rarified air. People thought I was special since I was his personal valet. I did nothing to dispel their assumptions. It was time to move forward and upward. In these three days, I met countless lawyers, businessmen, and politicians. It was the perfect environment for a student to be recruited for a dream job. In many of these places, I was the only student among all of these professionals. I decided to network the room, presenting myself in the best manner possible. I tried to act like I had been in this crowd of people my entire life. And, it worked. Over and over, I was handed business cards with a smile and a friendly invite: "Come see me, kid. We could use someone like you." Sometimes life is awesome.

In this newly discovered, magical world, I also met a stoic and affable man named Herb Gray. At the time, Mr. Gray was the longest standing politician in Canada. He had been in public office since 1962. I sat next to him during the night of the honorary dinner for the justice. We had an easy rapport. That evening he invited me to meet with him for a breakfast the next morning. I was busy with the justice but I agreed to meet him early, before the day filled.

We met and he wasted no time asking me if I wanted to join him in the world of politics. He explained to me that I had the perfect combination of presence, education, and cultural background for a tremendous career as a politician. It was very flattering but I told him that I wasn't interested in that type of work. Of course, at the time, I didn't actually know what I was saying "no" to. I knew absolutely nothing about politics other than all of the ugly signs they posted on front lawns every couple years. I knew he was important but I was too young and naïve to understand how rare an offer like this was.

Mr. Gray and I would continue a cordial relationship for about 10 years, meeting for meals or exchanging letters of correspondence with one another. A few years after our initial meeting, he became deputy prime minister of Canada. I visited him in Canada's capital, Ottawa. He smiled and said, "There's still room for you if you're interested." Unfortunately, I still had to pass. He was a good man.

Nonetheless, in early 1992, still in my surreal days, surrounded by luminaries and power, I was confused about my future. I now had too many options. In a matter of a couple years I had gone from killing chickens in my parents' basement to being courted by lawyers, businessmen, and politicians. I wasn't sure which path to take and I was still undecided about Russia. I owed them an answer. Two months had passed, and I had not responded to them. They tried to call me a couple of times, but I was too busy with all of the planning for the justice. I didn't like the notion of practicing law, but I really did like hanging out with all of these people. They treated me nicely and ate a lot of expensive food. I was certain that I could get a job with someone in the stack of business cards that were given to me. After all, that was the goal—to get a good job that brought in money. I was tired of having just enough to get by. And, I was certainly tired of being a student.

Then there was Justice Iacobucci. He was different than everyone else. He was engaging and welcoming with everyone he met, but it was almost as if he were invisible. By design, he blended seamlessly with whatever room he was in at the time.

We spent a lot of time together alone, and I filled it by asking him endless questions about his work. The most fascinating response for me was to the question, "How does it feel knowing that your decisions will affect the entire country?" Very patiently and calmly he replied, "It weighs on me heavily. It's a great responsibility. For that reason, I don't intend to be on the Supreme Court bench for longer than 10 years. The country needs perspectives other than mine." That was incredible to me. He had a lifetime appointment, but he was choosing to walk away after 10 years because he thought it was the right thing to do. This certainly was a different way of thinking than most lawyers I had met.

By the third day, I decided to tell him about my offer from the Russians. I also felt comfortable getting his opinion on law firms and perhaps the prospect of clerking for him at the Supreme Court of Canada. From my viewpoint, now was the time to get clarity. In my mind, there was no one better than him to give me an informed opinion on all of these areas. He understood the immigrant journey, the importance of education and prosperity. And, he understood the practice of law.

He listened patiently to all of my questions and then spoke to me about his life's path. He began by telling me that he wasn't a great student and that he was only able to get his first job at a law firm because his girlfriend was an excellent student. She told the law firm that if they wanted her, they needed to hire him as well. She would also later become his wife. He went on and on, telling me about all of the different jobs he had, including: a law school dean, in government, in private practice, etc. He then smiled and quoted a famous American lawyer, Oliver Wendell Holmes: "Anything is great if it is greatly pursued." He then told me to do whatever I wanted to do but just to be great at it.

I dropped him off at the airport and waved goodbye. Then I drove around the city for hours thinking about being great.

I woke up the next morning and thought, *If a Supreme Court judge is telling me that it's okay not to practice law, then it's okay. I'm going to try this business thing.*

Just like that, my life took another path and I would forgo a career in law. I would forgo the logical path to becoming the first lawyer in my family, forgo a possible job at the Supreme Court, and walk away from all of this certainty and prestige. Instead, I would start at the bottom again. Not just at the bottom of anywhere, but at the bottom in a former enemy country, located 5,000 miles away. It was a country in which people were starving and coup attempts had taken place; a country in which there was tremendous uncertainty, frustration, and anger amongst the people. It was also a place where that anger had boiled over and someone had already tried to stab me with a knife. Despite all of that, I still decided it was the better path. I saw opportunity and I was going to pursue it greatly.

I just had a few more obstacles in my great pursuit. For one thing, I had virtually no money, maybe a thousand dollars in my bank account. I had a part-time job, but I needed that money for daily expenses. I had a couple of department store credit cards but only with a $500 limit. I didn't speak Russian and I knew nothing of communism or Russian history. My potential partner and his friends knew nothing about capitalism. Their currency, the ruble, was not convertible on the open market; it could only be used in their country. And, most importantly, I knew nothing about starting or running a business—any business. I had no formal or practical business education other than a couple courses in economics. I had never taken accounting or finance courses. I had a degree in Sociology. I was a full-time law student and I was working part-time as an assistant childcare worker at the Children's Aid Society. Despite all of this, I thought, *Let's try.* It's amazing what you will do when you think you have nothing to lose. I actually had nothing physical to lose. If it didn't work out, I thought that I could always go practice law.

I would spend the next couple of months trying to figure out how to start a business, what to do, and how to get paid. I spent countless hours in libraries combing over textbooks on business as well as phone books. I researched everything I could and called anyone who might be able to help me start an international business. I knew nothing about banking and finance, so I visited a lot of bankers. I told them that I wanted to start a company and asked if I could borrow money to do so. They asked me about my collateral. I wasn't really sure what "collateral" meant because the only thing that I owned were milk crates full of books and a duffle bag of clothing. I had been in college for six years at that point, and I had just enough money to get by. Many of the bankers laughed at me but a few had sympathy. I would ask them for advice and they would say, "Do what you know." I was 24 and the only thing I knew about from being a student was pizza and beer.

After searching for options, I took the bankers' advice. I chose the most obvious path: I decided to export beer, meat, and cheese from North America to Russia. It was 1992, the time of long lines for bread and any kind of food. People were hungry, so it seemed like a good place to start—I would be matching a need in the business world with my "expertise."

The next challenge came in trying to figure out how we would actually buy this product. My contacts in Russia only had access to rubles, and that currency was only valid within their country. We explored different kinds of barter scenarios, but no one was interested. American beer companies didn't want to be paid in bee pollen—they wanted US funds.

At a certain point, I was ready to give up. We couldn't figure out how to buy the product—it was just too complicated. Finally, I said to my counterparts in Moscow, "If you want to do business here, you need to get me American dollars. I don't care how you do it, but that's the only way." I hung up thinking that was the end of my entrepreneurial adventure. Two weeks later, I received a fax from my partners in Russia that stated, "Check your bank account. Please tell us the amount of the wire that you received." I went to the bank and I was stunned. In my account was a deposit of $200,000. It was incredible. That account had never seen more than a couple of thousand dollars in all of my years as a student.

The next task brought another challenge. I thought it would be fun to spend $200,000, but it turned out to be a huge pain. I wanted to buy meat, but no one would take a meeting with me. No one took me seriously. The moment I said "Russia" people hung up. By this time in the economic cycle, there was a mad rush of companies trying to ship products to the former Soviet Union. Many were trying but many would fail, principally because of rampant theft and fraud. In the eyes of older businessmen, I was just a kid. They assumed there was no way I could be legitimate; I was either a con or I would *be* conned.

I decided to try another approach. It was time to be bold.

I put on a suit and tie, grabbed my briefcase, and drove to a food distributors' office in Detroit. It was located in a very rough part of town, and all of the crime associated with the crack cocaine epidemic was at its peak. This warehouse was surrounded by barbed wire, guard dogs, and security men. It was common that employees holstered guns to protect themselves. Getting mugged was a regular occurrence in this part of the city. Knowing all of this, I knew that it was a tough crowd. If I showed the least bit of indecisiveness, they wouldn't give me the time of day.

The receptionist was seated in a bulletproof glass case. Through the vent in the glass, I asked to speak to the head of sales, Michael. She asked if I had an appointment with him. I knew if I said "no," I would be asked to leave...so, I lied. "Yes, I have an appointment. My name is Domenic Aversa." She looked up and down her appointment schedule and didn't see my name. I said, "It must be a mix-up." She put her head down and continued to look for my name. I took a deep breath and thought, *I'm going for it*. I looked down the hallway at the security guard standing in the corner. He was holstering a very big gun and an even bigger nightstick. I looked at him, nodded my head as some sort of expression of agreement, and walked straight toward him. The receptionist raised her head and said something but the bulletproof glass muffled the sound. It didn't matter; I was moving fast. I was in dress shoes and my only thought at this point was that I won't be able to outrun the security guard when he's chasing me with that big, black nightstick. I reached the security guard, gave him a stern look, and said "hey" and then went through the next door. I just figured that I would keep walking until someone threw me out.

At each corner, with authority, I would ask, "Where's

Michael's office?" Someone would always diligently point toward a spot further down another hallway. After three turns, I walked into a very large room with approximately 30 desks, all facing forward. Salesmen were seated at each desk and were on the phone trying to hustle and sell meat. Every kind of meat possible; chicken, pork, beef, and every other creature that walked or flew. The back wall had a big white sign on it with a picture of a stout but cute pink pig. The caption on the sign read "We sell everything but the squeal." These were seriously aggressive salesmen.

There was a rapid, frenetic, and angry din to the entire room. Phones and desk drawers were constantly being slammed. Profanity rang through every conversation. "F you, I want half a penny a pound more." "F you, mother-f'rr. Suck this for your half penny. I'll give you a quarter penny if you lick my sister's ass." This was definitely not a place for tea and scones. I think if you said the wrong thing to that crowd, they might just sell you to a butcher and no one would be the wiser.

At the first desk I saw where someone wasn't sweating animal blood, I stopped and again asked for Michael. The slovenly gentleman simply pointed to the front of the room.

Standing behind a big oak desk, there was a slender, middle-aged, average-height guy talking into one phone with another phone slung over his other shoulder. He spoke in a low tone in short and fast bursts. All I heard was, "No." "Is that it?" "Just do what I'm telling you." "F you if you don't want to be my customer. That's the price." This is how he talked with customers; imagine how he talked to his employees?

He looked miserable and mean. It's as if he was just waiting for an excuse to take your head off. As I approached his desk, I saw that he was holstering a gun on his belt on his left hip. I slowed my pace, stopped directly in front of him, and just stared at him. Still on the phone, he looked at me, up and down. We were both dressed in blue, only he in jeans and me in a suit. His expression then turned to somewhere between contempt and disgust. Without further examination or delay, he cupped his hand over the receiver and asked, "Can I help you?" I replied, "Yes. I would like to buy some meat from you." He gave me a scowl, then looked away and returned to his phone. I shook my head in disbelief. How hard could it be to spend money?

I pushed aside the papers he was looking at on his desk with my hand, put my briefcase down, opened it, pulled out a cashier's check for $50,000, handed it to him, and asked, "Is this enough?" He put down both phones and just continued to stare at the check. He was dumbfounded. I said, "It's real." And he said, "Oh, I know. I just don't know who you are. What kind of lunatic walks around this neighborhood with a $50,000 cashier's check?" I then told him who I was, and he responded with, "Oh, the Russia kid. Where did you get the money? Are you a gangster?" I smiled and said, "My grandmother left it for me. What do you care where I got the money? Do you want to sell me meat or should I go to your competitor?" Without missing a beat, he said, "Have a seat, kid. I will sell you whatever you want." Michael and I would go on to be good friends. By far, one of the sharpest and hardworking people I ever met. When you spoke with him he would say, "Okay, I have just enough time between the raindrops to talk with you. What's on your mind?"

My experience with Michael taught me to be bold and quick and speak with cash. I would repeat the same technique with the beer and cheese companies in Illinois and Wisconsin until, finally, we had full containers and we were ready to ship. We coordinated the entire process; purchasing, packaging, insurance, shipping, storage, distribution, sales. It was a lot to learn. I spent countless hours on the phone learning the different terminology, reviewing all of the contracts and then explaining it to my Russian partners. I knew very little about business other than "make a profit." My partners knew very little about capitalism other than "make a profit." But, somehow, we inched along doing what seemed best at the time.

Everything seemed to be perfect and on schedule for the first big shipment until all of it was stopped at the Finland/Russia border. Apparently, they had found all kinds of problems with our paperwork. We spent several days trying to sort through the issues until one of my Russian partners realized there was no problem. The real issue was money; the border agents wanted a pay-out. With the prospect of losing everything, we were left with no choice; we sent someone there with a couple of envelopes filled with cash and magically our paperwork was resolved.

We were able to sell all of our product and turn a modest profit, but I still wasn't convinced that this new venture would be a great success. Many of the same challenges still existed, and I still needed to finish law school. Trying to get a business in Moscow off the ground was time-consuming and expensive. The phone bills alone were overwhelming. I decided that I needed more money to put toward the business. I was committed and prepared to find every spare penny I could. So, I moved back in with my parents to save on rent money and groceries. My parents thought I was crazy but they were supportive. They didn't understand how I could go to school and operate a business on the other side of the world at the same time. Quite frankly, neither did I. I just kept working at both.

My father and I built an office in the basement. It was located right next to the wine and food cellar and directly across from the laundry room. It had no windows, but I did have two phone lines installed. One for a fax, one for an actual phone. My dad felt that I needed some movement of air, so he installed a vent in the ceiling. Somehow, at 24, I didn't think oxygen was important. Glad I had my father looking out for me.

Over the course of the coming year, I would essentially live in that office. I would call my partners in Moscow generally around 9 p.m. or 10 p.m. and I would talk with them and work until 3 a.m. I would go to bed and then I'd get up and go to classes around 8 a.m. They were long days, but I slept soundly and I had a lot of fun.

It was by far the most interesting office I ever had. The smell alternated between prosciutto and wine from the cellar to laundry detergent from the washing machine. Since I belonged to a big Italian family that was surrounded by an even bigger Italian community, there was always someone visiting. Almost daily, there was a stampede taking place over my head from all of the feet walking back and forth in that small house. And at least twice per week there were four to eight different people over for dinner. I was constantly surrounded by a boisterous but delicious-smelling environment. Nevertheless, I stayed focused. I stayed locked in my windowless room trying to become "something." I wasn't entirely sure that I knew what I was doing, but I knew that things were getting done and we were starting to make real money.

So, what did I do with my first bucket of money? What

would a formerly economically challenged and basement-dwelling, 25-year-old son of immigrants buy with his first serious paycheck? A car? A house? A boat? Nope. I bought a professional soccer team. Yes, you read that sentence correctly; a soccer team.

The Windsor Wheels played in the Canadian National Soccer League. I had played soccer for eight years in my youth so, in my mind, when I was presented with the opportunity to buy the team, I thought it would be fun. At this point in my life, I saw no limits to anything. I was pursuing greatness. In my mind, everything was possible and business was just like the carnival; colorful, unpredictable, and exciting. To make matters more interesting, I didn't just buy any team; I bought a team that had not won a game in two years. Why make things easy on myself? Not only did I have our business in Russia but I had three more months left in law school and now I owned a losing team whose opening day was four months away. It was illogical and improbable but I did it anyhow.

I purchased the team with two other partners based in Michigan. The plan was to buy this team in Canada and then buy the future rights to a team in Michigan before the onset of Major League Soccer in the US. The Canadian team would be a feeder team for the larger, US-based team. However, the distance between what we bought and where we wanted to go was significant. With our purchase price came the name and rights to the team – that's it. We had no coach, no stadium, and no players. We didn't even have a soccer ball. We had to build the team from bottom up. What did I know about running a professional sports franchise? Nothing. What did my partners know? A little more than nothing. Seemed like the perfect place to start.

We decided that we only had so much money to spend. We could either try to recruit and pay great players or we could spend everything on marketing, building prestige and fun around the team to draw a base of fans. We went with marketing. One by one, we met with potential players. One by one, we told them our vision and asked them to give us one year with no salary but in that year they would receive first-class treatment every day. We would put them in the best hotels, best buses, and planes. Have the finest uniforms and eat five-star food before and after each practice and game. We promised them that they would feel like champions.

The message worked. One by one, they signed with us. Our recruiting accelerated once we signed a new coach. We were lucky; he was a friend of one of my partners. He was in between work. He had just finished up as head coach for the men's soccer team at Rutgers University. He had also played in a European league in previous years. He was the consummate soccer fanatic. His entire life was soccer. He jumped into the process with maniacal passion, and within a couple weeks he assembled a team of players from around the world. We had 15 guys from 12 different countries: England, Holland, Portugal, Italy, Croatia, Hungary, Turkey, Uganda, Jamaica, Brazil, and, of course, the United States and Canada. It was an actual melting pot of diversity. Some of them were first-rate players; most were second or third tier – but I didn't care. They were passionate, colorful, and skilled just enough that I knew we could light up the field and entertain people. And we did just that.

We won our opening game, our first win in two years, defeating the defending champions from the previous year, 4-0. They never saw us coming. They expected a ragtag bunch by an owner who was just a 25-year-old kid. However, what they got was a dose of lightning and toughness. I was at every practice and every meal, spoke with every player, constantly looking for ways to improve and gel as a team. With this big win, I was convinced we would be a powerhouse. It didn't take long to crush that notion.

We lost the next five games. The Windsor Wheels were in dead last, again.

A few days after the fifth loss, two guys from one of the other teams in the league showed up to our practice. One was very tall, the other very short. One was a goalie, the other a midfielder. They approached me on the field and said, "Hi, Domenic. Tony told us to tell you that we play for you now." What? "That's crazy. This has to be a joke. I can't afford to pay you guys." They shrugged their shoulders and said, "Well, Tony said we have to play for you for the rest of the season." This was nuts. They lived four hours away. What was I going to do with these guys?

Tony, their team owner, had immigrated from Italy in the late 1950s. He still had an accent when he spoke but he loved his life in Canada. He had become wealthy owning several auto body repair shops. Tony was also chairman of the league. He and I had become friendly after an initial awkward first meeting. I walked into the boardroom for an owners' preseason meeting. Before I could take my seat, he asked, "Where's yo' daddy?" He was under the impression that an older gentleman had bought the team. He had only reviewed our purchase agreement, not actually met with us. When I told him that I was the actual owner, he shook his head and said, "Impossible, you justa young boy." I smiled and said, "It's very possible. I'm not so young. I'm 25. It's my money and my team. Can we start the meeting?"

Now, six games into the season and in last place, I called

Tony about these two players. "Tony, did you send your guys here?" "Yeah, you needa goalie and midfielder o' you nevva gunna win." "I can't afford to pay them?" "That's okay. I like you. I'm gunna pay them. You just go do yo' best." And he hung up.

He was right. With those two changes we went on a serious winning streak. We won the next eight games. By midseason, we were tied for first place.

It was an amazing time. I was having a blast. It was pure showtime. We had fireworks, bands, and cheerleaders. Anything I could give away free, I would. I just wanted people to have a good time. At the beginning of each game, I had players run out of the lockers with handfuls of long-stem roses. I had them run into the stands to hand them out to all of the women, young and old alike. At the same time I had other guys run beside them to hand out gifts such as mini soccer balls to all of the young boys. I wined and dined everyone. After each home game, I would invite the visiting team and their staff and families to a restaurant for dinner. I thought business was about making friends and having fun. To me, there's no place better to accomplish this than over a great meal. Soon, as we travelled, every team in the league started reciprocating our offer. Every city we played in, win or lose, we always ended the evening in a party as guests of the other owner.

I was always looking for new ways to get the team more fans and more exposure. At the beginning of the season, we handed out more than 3,000 free season passes to kids under the age of 12. We needed people in the stands. Fans brought sponsors; sponsors brought legitimacy. We also cut a deal with the local cable TV station to have all of our games, including those in other cities, broadcast several times. We lived in a city where many people did shift work in factories so they may miss games. I was adamant about building a following. So, I offered to pay for all of their broadcasters' and crew's travel expenses. They travelled right next to us for the entire season. And, in exchange, our games were televised three and sometimes four times through a weekend. I then could tell sponsors that they would get six to eight hours of television time each week. It was a great deal for them and us.

All of this was fast and exciting but nothing was more fun than when I created an advertisement for Lotto, our clothing and shoe sponsor, where the central image would be the team posing in the nude. Adidas, Lotto's primary rival in soccer apparel, a week earlier had run an ad in *Sports Illustrated* with one of our competitors in the Canadian National Soccer League. In this ad, the players were entirely nude but for their shoes. In 1993, it caused a tremendous uproar. Many people were offended but many others loved it. Whatever it was, it was exposure. I saw the commotion and thought, *We can do this…but we'll do it better.* So, I put each player in a long-tail tuxedo jacket, bow tie, cummerbund, and Lotto cleats, and gave each of them a long stem red rose to cover their private parts. Then, just before the photographer started to shoot, I decided to join in. I took off all of my clothes, grabbed a tux and a rose, and smiled for the camera. Why not?

I couldn't convince the Lotto executives in Dallas to run the ad in *Sports Illustrated*. They were far more conservative than Adidas. However, they did give me permission to run the ad in a smaller sports publication in Canada. My mother tried hard to be proud of me, but for a while it was a difficult conversation with her friends. "So, your son graduated from law school, isn't practicing law... but he's posing half-nude in magazines?"

By the time the season ended, we had slipped back to fourth place, but we made it all the way to the semifinals of the Canadian Cup. We were two wins away from a big shiny trophy; from the outhouse to penthouse in one season. The top of the mountain was right there within our reach. It was the most fun I have ever had in business. I didn't make a dollar of profit but the entire experience was thoroughly enjoyable.

By this time, my business in Russia was really growing. It grew so quickly that I decided that I needed to give up the soccer team. At the end of the season, I gave my shares to my two partners. It was a sad farewell.

Now, focused solely on our efforts in Russia, I could concentrate on our ever-expanding company. Within a year, we were shipping millions of dollars' worth of product. We took our profits and started a finance company. It was a very basic formula; we would lend money to other small businesses. Concurrently, to take advantage of all of the dramatic changes in the community in Moscow, we started a construction business, overhauling private residences for commercial space.

It was a very dynamic and rewarding time. I went from college student to international businessman in a very short period of time. I traded in my eight-year-old pair of jeans and tattered sweatshirt for tailor-made clothes. I flew first-class and read papers like *The European* and *South China Daily*. I had accountants and lawyers working for me in three different countries. I was quickly learning the ins and outs of being "multi-national."

The environment in Moscow also changed rapidly. The

"New Rich" started to appear. Restaurants, nightclubs, hotels, and clothing stores popped up. Everything was new, and nothing was understated. People had lived in a subdued and subservient manner for so long that everyone wanted to make a statement. Color and life appeared. It felt just like it actually was; like we were all watching and helping a brand-new world be created.

Unfortunately, as wealth grew, so did violence. Money poured into the country but only in the hands of a small group. The rest of the country was improving, but they were still very poor. The Brave New World was now becoming the Wild Wild East. It was a lawless land—anything that wasn't nailed down was stolen. Ships were being commandeered in the ports and entire trains were being robbed. They would steal refrigerated containers, plug them in, and use them as storefronts. To keep our shipments from being delayed or stolen each week, one of our secretaries would make a round of deliveries of white envelopes. Everyone from the harbor master to the head of immigration, police officers, and security guards received cash in an envelope. It was pure survival; we had to pay people not to steal our stuff.

Many people were still struggling, and it was a competition for their services. If we didn't pay them, thieves would pay them to turn a blind eye. We didn't bring them a lot of money, but it had to be there every week. At that time, a police officer made approximately $25 a month. By doubling his monthly salary each week, we were protecting hundreds of thousands of dollars of product. It seemed like a good deal to me.

Theft among citizens and business was serious, but within banks it was far more rampant and devious. Across the entire Soviet Union, loan documents were being forged and wire transfers were manipulated. The IMF (International Monetary Fund) and World Bank were pouring billions into the CIS, hoping that it would not revert back to communism. But the money, mostly unaccounted for, left as fast as it came in. Aspiring businessmen would borrow millions with no experience, no collateral, and just a bit of a kickback to the lender, and then they would disappear. They would take the money with no intention of ever paying it back. Many of them moved to the best beach cities around the world. This was their free ticket out of the cold; literally and figuratively.

As a company, our security detail also grew. We had a small army guarding our warehouse of goods 24/7. We also had security guards for each of us. At this time, guns were everywhere: underneath the seats of our cars, in our offices, and in everyone's briefcase or purse. There were so many guns around that I made a decision to never carry one. I didn't have a moral problem with having a gun; I just was afraid that I might actually use it on someone. It was a forced discipline; it made me be more careful about how I spoke and how I carried myself. The memory of the old man trying to stab me for being loud never left me.

I can't say that this world became normal to me, but I grew accustomed to it. Most meetings consisted of a table full of men who were either hungover or steeped in vodka, and everyone holstered a gun. I learned to speak carefully, slowly, and in a moderated tone. I knew that one wrong inflection and someone would put their finger on the trigger. It was crazy, but I was solely focused on making my business grow. I knew what it was like to be broke and if this was the path out, so be it.

In addition to not carrying a weapon, I also made another important decision: never promise what I couldn't deliver. We were surrounded by so much lying, cheating, and deception that I just decided I wasn't going to get caught up in it. In fact, I didn't even want to get close to the typical businessman conversation. In the Wild Wild East, everyone bragged, exaggerated, and promised something. Anything and everything seemed possible, but of course, it wasn't. It was a developing country that was in the middle of a cultural, political, and economic revolution. There was constant chaos. No one, not even those in power, knew what the next day would bring.

I wasn't raised in the Soviet Union, but I grew up around a lot of people who struggled and worked hard for what little they had. They were tough. Most of my friends and the entire neighborhood were European immigrants who had arrived in Canada when they were broke and looking for work. Everyone had been involved with WWII in one way or another; losing side, winning side—it didn't matter. Everyone had suffered through the war. This made people hard. Certainly, everyone was friendly and generous but the moment something was out of line, anger rose quickly.

You learned not to screw up, cheat, lie, and steal. Or, at least not to get caught doing any of those things. Parents gave teachers permission to hit their kids if they misbehaved. Some parents gave neighbors the same leeway. Living in my neighborhood at times felt like living during the Crusades or The Inquisition. It was an enclave of Christians, centered by a Catholic grade school. All filled with tightly wound, angry people looking for a fight. I don't think there was a two-week period of time through eight years of grade school where someone didn't hit me. I don't think I was alone in this, but it certainly was a highlight in my youth. I was a good student but I was always taking chances, I was always exploring.

When you do that, you're going to stand out and you're going to be perceived as breaking rules. I was curious about science so I asked about evolution; my teacher, a properly smocked nun, proceeded to beat me with the chalk brush and then throw me out of the class. On another occasion, I threw a snowball at another student, which earned me a beating with a leather strap from the school principal. Then, there was the day I forgot to bring homework to my desk mate who was at home ill; that entitled me to be beaten with a stack of books over my head by my 240-pound teacher. And, of course, there was the time that I walked across a neighbor's yard one too many times, which entitled me to be whipped with the branch from a willow tree from that elderly, sweet neighbor. I was hit by everyone with everything: belts, brooms, shoes, bats, pieces of lumber. I didn't care. The more they hit, the more resilient I became. I didn't know any better. I thought this was how the world worked: break the rules; take a beating.

Since our parents, teachers, and all the adults around us acted in this manner, this is how we acted amongst friends. We were close, we played, we shared, but when something went wrong, there wasn't a long discussion about it. We didn't chitchat; we settled matters with fists. What was the least desired trait? Lying. If you were a perpetual bullshitter, in short order someone would punch you in the mouth. That sting and those few drops of blood would help you think twice about what you said next time.

For me, Russia was no different than where I grew up, except that the punch to the face would be replaced by a bullet to the head. So, it was an easy decision: always speak simply and honestly. This one decision would help keep me alive since I was surrounded by criminals. Disputes always arose but, over time, they knew that whatever I represented was the truth.

The level of violence rose to such an extent that some of the higher-end restaurants installed metal detectors. Before passing through the machines, people would check their guns at the door and then wrap their claim tickets around their bullets. Most of the men would put the bullets in the breast pocket of their suits and then head off to dinner.

Most meals were fun and filled with excitement. Everyone was making money and the room was adorned with conspicuous wealth. Everything was new and colorful, but the backdrop was always dangerous. It was still a society struggling to find itself, and with the changes came a fight for power. It was a time when the price of life was cheap; you could have a man killed for $500. Each night, as you scanned the room, it became easier to tell who was a criminal: pretty much everyone.

In October 1993, I was in the US and we had some important meetings scheduled in Moscow. We knew that the country was still unsettled, and many hardline communists wanted their old country back. The ones who had not become businessmen or criminals were out of power. The Communist Party had been dissolved and many didn't know what to do with their new lives as commoners. It appeared that another coup attempt was imminent. Despite knowing this, I flew to Russia for the meetings. Sure enough, less than 12 hours after landing, the Parliament building had been overtaken and set on fire. Tanks and militiamen were moving swiftly through the streets.

It was a Sunday and we were at a *dacha* (vacation home) in the countryside with most of our employees and some of their families, enjoying a barbequed meal and a healthy amount of vodka. It was relaxing and fun. At one point, we turned up the music and everyone danced. It seemed like happy days were definitely here to stay. But, that thought was short-lived. As the sun set, we received a phone call that things were turning ugly in the city. Upon hearing this news, we immediately went separate ways. My partners went into hiding; they were considered capitalist traitors and would certainly be the first target of the hardliners. I knew that it was a volatile time, so before we went out to the countryside, I taped my passport, my return airplane ticket, and a thousand dollars in cash to my left arm. I needed to be prepared for an emergency. I returned to my hotel, ready to leave the country or get to the Canadian Embassy.

Once in my hotel room, I turned on CNN™. I watched men with machine guns randomly shooting people, and I watched as the Parliament building, only a few blocks away from my hotel, was surrounded by tanks. Knowing my parents were also probably watching, I phoned them to let them know that I was safe. As I was on the phone with my mother, I heard gunfire outside of my window. I was on the third floor. I peered around the curtains to see a man spraying the hotel with bullets. At the same time, I saw this exact image on the TV screen. I looked back out the window and I saw the CNN™ cameraman further back. The hardline rebel then began to shoot upwards, toward me. In that instance, as my mother was asking me, "What's all of that noise?" I was watching a man shoot at me on TV just outside of my window. "Nothing, Mom. It's just CNN™." Fortunately, he got bored and moved on. I didn't sleep a minute that night.

Somewhere between 900-2,000 people were killed in that uprising. Eventually, the dust settled, and the hardliners lost. Capitalism, democracy, and newly minted criminals won. They were the foundation of the future.

We road that wave of success and continued to expand our business throughout the former Soviet Union. We were looking at building subdivisions, golf resorts, and a marina; we were negotiating to have all of our beer manufactured exclusively at our own facility in the Czech Republic; and our finance company had grown to the point where we applied and qualified as a licensed commercial bank. This was a huge success. In my mind, I was conquering. I was building an empire. I spent many days reading about Andrew Carnegie, J. D. Rockefeller, Henry Ford, and JP Morgan. I thought I was a new industrialist. And if I had any doubt, I just read more books by authors such as Tony Robbins, Brian Tracey, Zig Ziglar, and Wayne Dyer. This was the '90s; everything was possible. Whatever I could dream of, I could achieve. I could own many banks, many buildings, many ships, many businesses. There was no limit. I just had to believe, repeat it, and act as if it already had happened. I would awaken the giant inside of me and turn everything I touched into gold. I was absolutely convinced that as we marched toward the 21st century, I was reliving what it was like to be living at the end of the 19th century in America. That was a period of great change, excitement, and newfound wealth. Now it was happening in Russia and there I was—in on the ground floor. I was certain that I would become a titan of industry and commerce.

Then, one day, my partner was confronted by two men outside of our office in Moscow. One of them held a medium-sized, black leather duffle bag. He opened the bag to show my partner its contents. It was filled with clay-based explosives. As my partner looked in the bag, one of the men said, "We will blow up your building, kill all of your employees, kill your families, and then the three of you." Ordinary crime had just reached an extraordinary level.

We had received word from one adversary that we needed to get out of the banking business. We were told that we could keep our food and real estate endeavors, but banking was to cease. I was a businessman; I just wanted to make money. I had no interest in fighting anyone. I thought that having two out of three businesses was fine. I was disappointed, but I didn't fret because there were so many other opportunities that we could pursue. My partners saw it differently, however. They were Russian. They had grown up in a more privileged world in the Soviet Union. They were well-educated, well-connected, and had no intention of giving in to this group. They just viewed them as another business obstacle. Unfortunately, this group decided to be very precise in their negotiations. They intended to make a statement by blowing up our office and killing everyone associated with us.

Despite my pleading, my partners dug in their heels. To me, it was clear; if I fought back, I would have to kill people. The moment I did that, I would be a criminal and there would be no turning back from that life. It was a struggle for power and I was willing to concede. I just wanted to be a businessman; mobster wasn't on the agenda.

Before we could deliver an answer, we received their response. One of my partner's homes was completely shredded by machine gun fire and he and his family had disappeared. We weren't certain if he had escaped or whether he had been kidnapped or killed. We decided to send all of our employees' home. My other partner went into hiding, and I buried myself in my office in the States.

I didn't have any books that prepared me for being hunted. I just sat and waited for the smoke to clear or to be killed. Within a couple of days, just as I had expected, two men showed up outside of my home. They sat in their car each night, all night, and just watched me. I didn't leave the house.

On the third day, I sent messages to Moscow and to all of our employees that we were closing up all of our businesses, including the food and real estate divisions. I immediately wired out any outstanding monies that we owed or had borrowed. I cleaned out our accounts, paying everyone that I could.

My remaining partner was very upset with me and we argued about staying in business. We didn't need the bank to be in business; we had a food import company and a real estate development company that were doing very well. We had worked hard to get to this point. He didn't see why we had to dismantle all of it, and he was right; we didn't. But I knew that if I stayed, I would be facing this decision again— kill or be killed—and that wasn't what I wanted. I considered myself lucky to be alive, so now it was time to leave.

Within a short while of emptying our accounts, the men in the car outside of my home left. Despite my partner's pleas, I don't think that I would have made it to the end of the sidewalk if I had decided to stay in any business. I think we were marked and now perceived as weak. This time it was about banking; next time it would be about something else they wanted. It was just best to end everything.

I unplugged my phones, threw away all my mail, and avoided people for weeks. It took me a long time to absorb what had actually happened. I was fortunate to still be alive.

I was also fortunate to have some money saved and put aside. I didn't leave emptyhanded.

Despite the brushes with danger in Russia, it all became very real when it arrived on my doorstep in the United States. All of a sudden, it wasn't a great exploration. It wasn't just business. I was playing with fire in my own home. I tried to build a legitimate business in a world dominated by crime. I thought that I could manage through the danger, violence, and corruption and somehow come out unscathed. I thought that the trouble and violence were "over there," in another box, in a far-away land, being caused by other people. I was honest and honored all of my agreements, and I thought that was enough to keep me safe and above all of the rest—but it wasn't. I learned that if you're in the room and trouble is happening and you say nothing, you are part of the problem. It was a hard lesson, but I learned that there is no way of going into a sewer without getting stink on you.

The idea of being the only gentleman in a room filled with liars and thieves was a childish, romantic notion. Rockefeller, Carnegie, and Morgan all left a trail of blood and corruption on their upward paths to success. I knew it; I just chose to forget it. To me, their stories were more grandiose without the messy parts. It's easy to forget about the manure in the soil when you're sipping champagne. I had been living the high life for years at a very young age. I thought that I had tiptoed through all of the landmines and that I was safe. I was counting money long before it came in, and I had no reason to believe it would ever end. I couldn't have been more wrong.

By 1998, 80% of all commercial banks in Russia were controlled by the mafia. They were smart mobsters; instead of shaking down each business, they went right to the primary financial source. By controlling the banks, they had access to all of the personal and commercial finances of everyone living or doing business in Russia. They had a grand plan and I wasn't part of it. Even if I had decided to fight back, there was no way I would have ever won that war.

So, this is life. This is *business* life. It's full of ups and downs. When business goes well, we feel great. When it fails, we feel terrible and want to hide. If we're honest with ourselves, we know the mistakes we made. The hard part is actually changing our behavior, so we don't repeat the mistakes. I was still too young and naïve to fully comprehend what I had been through, but I knew that I wasn't dead, so I had to do something. The question was, *what would I do next?* I was 28 years old and had already lived a life most could never imagine. Where could I go after walking that high-wire act in the Wild Wild East?

Despite having graduated from law school, I still had no interest in practicing law. Dozens of lawyers had worked for me in the past few years and I still saw the practice as glorified playtime; a bunch of people playing with words and phrases. I thought they were important, but I still had a yearning to create and build. I decided, therefore, to learn more about running an actual business. I had built up my first company with a great deal of enthusiasm, moxie, and luck. I had learned a few things from all of the people I had met, but I felt that it wasn't enough to be truly great in business; I felt that I needed to learn a lot more technical aspects such as accounting, finance, and engineering.

I found a consulting company that was listed on *Inc.* magazine's list of the fastest growing companies in America. It sold typical management consulting services but in a very atypical way. Rather than using networks in the country club and college alumni groups, its business model involved going door-to-door selling advice. It took a high-brow line of work and made it very reachable for the masses and, in a matter of a few years, they went from $250K in revenue to $50M. I was fascinated, and I wanted to learn, so I took a job as a business analyst with them.

Consulting work at this firm was sold in three stages: (i) a salesman would sell an assessment; (ii) an analyst would sell consulting services; and (iii) consultants would work and bill for those services. My job was to go into a company and analyze as much of it as I could in one to two days. I had a maximum of 48 hours to dissect every aspect of a company, identify problems, suggest solutions, sell them a consulting project, and get them to sign a contract. I sold as I always did, by being straightforward. I would map out inconsistencies in their business and show them how they could make more money and have an easier workday. Just like Russia, it was all about building trust. The only difference was that I had less than 48 hours to build that trust. It seems crazy to jump into a business relationship that deep that quickly, but I loved it. There was no time for talk about sports and weather. We went right into the most sensitive parts quickly. I got to look into every private aspect of a company including their financials, production, and distribution. I got to speak candidly to owners, employees, customers, and suppliers. Oftentimes, I spoke to spouses who were part-owners but were never at the company, and to parents, cousins, silent partners, bankers, lawyers, accountants, friends, and neighbors. I was doing investigative analysis at rapid speed.

The company I worked for was incredibly sharp. They were able to move fast because they had developed systems. They took the mystery out of business; everything was in buckets and formulas. They gave me countless binders full of questions to ask, charts to fill, and presentations to prepare, and everything was done by hand. For me, this was a godsend. It was structure and knowledge that I was desperately seeking. I just did exactly as they told me; I asked every question, calculated every formula, and filled in every presentation.

The principal owner and CEO of this company was an inimitable and brilliant man. However, he had flexible morals. When I first met him, I asked him a question regarding what we should do if we found illegal activities at a client's place of business. I wanted to know how we should address it. He responded by saying, "There are black areas, white areas, and gray areas. We don't want to break the law; we just want to make the gray areas bigger." I should have left the company as soon as I heard that answer, but I didn't. It was a unique environment and I was learning a lot. I hadn't witnessed an illegal activity or behavior, so I brushed it off as colorful nonsense.

However, I would then come to learn that this CEO had been disbarred for mismanagement of client trust funds, and then his broker's license was revoked for commodities trading violations. I no longer thought that he was waxing poetically when he answered my question. He was fast and slick and had clearly broken laws in the past, in the legal and stock market communities. Yet now he was being featured on the cover of magazines and posing with the president and presidential candidates. I thought, *Maybe he's changed. Let's see what happens.* The moment that I have concrete proof of bad behavior, I'll leave.

Aside from his prior, criminal conduct, he was an astute study of human nature. He was relentless about two things:

having people focus on their job and feeding their greatest desires.

He held three sales meetings per day for all of the senior managers at the corporate headquarters. He set sales targets and reviewed progress at 8 a.m., noon, and 3 p.m. There were no quarterly, monthly, or weekly meetings; there were three per day. If there was a problem, you had three to four hours to fix it. He drove business like Patton drove tanks across a battlefield. If you cried, complained, or were confused, you were gone. The only department that was busier than sales was human resources. He didn't worry about conducting a lot of interviews to find the "right" person. His philosophy was to cast the net wide and often, bring all the catch on board, and throw out anyone who couldn't survive. Essentially, if you had a suit and were semi-literate, you got a job. Of course, somewhere around 90% of the new hires never lasted more than a week, but if he found one new shark, he felt his goal had been achieved.

If you worked at the main office, he expected your undivided attention all day. To help facilitate this, he had runners—full-time staff to accommodate the full-time staff. They brought lunch to them, picked up their dry-cleaning, did their grocery shopping, took their kids to soccer practice, and even picked up their in-laws from the airport. He took away every excuse for not being able to get the job done. When people started to burn out and expressed frustration about fatigue, spouses, or family, he was right there to soothe them. He'd ask, "What do you want?" and there was nothing forbidden on the list. Without missing a beat he'd ask, "Do you want to go somewhere? Vegas? The Caribbean? I'll have you on a flight tonight." If that wasn't enough, he'd continue. "You want a new car? Go to Ferrari. Pick out the one you want. It's done." "Still not enough? Is your wife upset? Your kids don't listen to you? How about a new house? Let's get you a new house. Go find one this weekend. Call my banker, and I'll take care of everything. Okay? Life is easy. Get what makes you happy. You deserve to be happy."

He held true to his word. The parking lot was filled with high-end cars and everyone lived in great neighborhoods. He would finance everything; he'd make all the arrangements, take on all of the payments, and then, eventually, he would take it out of their paychecks. No one cared, though. It was a drug-dealing type of management style. They asked for it, and he made it happen. He fed their addictions to power and possessions. He knew that everyone loves to feel rich and special. I'm not sure if it was moral or immoral. He promised and delivered the American dream just like everyone else— he just delivered it faster.

Were there occasions when I felt that he and others were pushing the line of morality and criminality? Yes. I couldn't put my finger on one specific thing that I heard that was criminal, but I knew that eventually they would get there. If your belief system is to constantly test limits and make "gray areas bigger," you will eventually cross the line. Despite all of this, I was taken in by the intelligence, acumen, speed, and dynamic environment. Once again, I was seduced by my desire to grow and learn. For some reason, I thought that this would be different than Russia; there were no guns or coup attempts. It was America, so there were established laws and structure. I put my head down, planning to stay in my own lane and insulate myself from my colleagues. So, with this in mind, I went and raced at breakneck speed.

Conducting the assessments was fascinating, but the travel involved in the work was grueling. I would be in two or three different cities each week, and I was taking three to six planes per week. I covered anywhere in North America east of the Mississippi. There was no rhyme or reason to the types of businesses I analyzed. They included car dealerships, grain elevator operators, lighting boutiques, pharmacists, security alarm companies, decorative stones, jewelers, dentists, auto parts distributors, graphic designers, and on and on.

There were no restrictions on where we would travel to work with a company. For some reason, I seemed to get assigned a lot of work in small towns. Places where they might not have access to the best financial or managerial advisors. Nonetheless, wherever it was, I had to find it and be ready to work. Which wasn't always easy. This was a long time before GPS and hotels.com, and everything was done by phone and Rand McNally map. Long gone were my tailor-made suits and sports cars. Five-star hotels and private security guards were nowhere to be found. I went back to complete basics: two suits—one blue, the other... blue; three shirts, all white; and one pair of black shoes. The company gave me $120 per day, per diem. I had $120 a day for a room, a car, and food, and I had to book all of this on my own, always at the last minute. For example, I would finish a job on a Tuesday at 5 p.m. in Georgia and then I would find out that I was starting my next job in Minnesota on Wednesday at 8 a.m. I would have about 12 hours to catch a plane, get a car, find the business, get a hotel, eat, press my suit and shirt, and then sleep. Rarely did I get more than a few hours of sleep.

I stayed in dozens of genuine fleabag motels. In these instances, I would shower, shave, press my clothes, get dressed, and sleep fully clothed and ready to go for the morning. It was just easier to pretend that I was on a layover in an airport rather than to accept the disgusting surroundings.

A handful of times I slept in my car. Anyone who has ever done this knows it's not fun in the least. One time I couldn't find a hotel; it was below zero outside and I was desperate for sleep. I found the client's business around 11 p.m. and there was a cleaning staff working inside. Out of sheer exhaustion, I went into one of the offices, put two chairs together, and slept there. Somewhere around 4 a.m. I found a bathroom, shaved, and made myself look presentable before anyone else showed up.

Dining was not much better. Most days I would end up eating at some gas station—either Chez BP or Chez Shell. I had to make it a game or it would be too disheartening. I had to forget the past and focus on what I was learning. I carried around a Pocket MBA and each day I would try to memorize new formulas. I also kept reading textbooks on accounting and finance. Then, each day, I went from company to company.

After months of doing dozens of assessments I learned about the importance of keeping an open mind throughout the entire process. I learned that the story you hear on the first day is very different than the story you hear on the second day. On the first day, the owner, CEO, CFO, or other C-level executive would show you reports and give organized explanations for their problems, successes, and challenges. On the next day, generally the day I would speak with all the other employees and conduct company-wide confidential surveys, I would get an entirely different picture. The closer I could get to employees, the more stories I would hear. This included all the dirt—where they cut corners, who came in late, who was having an affair, which supplier was screwing up but was a relative or friend, gambling debts, drug addictions, cars, boats, secret apartments, jealousy, hatred. It was all there; the frailty of human nature.

So, I learned to keep gathering information, but I also learned that business is generally straightforward. It's the people who make it complicated. I concluded that there are three critical questions for every business: (i) What is most important to the customer? (ii) What drives productivity? and (iii) What drives profitability? Once you answer those, you're off to a good start. The rest is all about managing people. If you can minimize all the typical human entanglements in the workplace, you have improved your odds for success dramatically.

There is one example from my time as an analyst that stands out in my memory with regard to dealing with complicated, difficult people. I was in Philadelphia analyzing a security alarm business. The owner was crisp. His shirts were heavily starched, and his office was pristinely organized. Every question I asked was answered sharply and cordially. There was only one problem: everyone was terrified of him. There were many problems in the business, but nothing could change because everyone was afraid to confront him. Anyone who challenged him was ridiculed and then fired.

I thought, *No problem; we just need to talk through this.* I asked his most trusted senior advisors if they would like to voice their suggestions with me present, and I would act as the moderator and facilitator. All three advisors agreed, so I called a meeting in the boardroom with all of us and the owner. One by one, I asked each one of them for suggestions on how the business could be improved. Each spoke carefully but openly, and the owner sat at the end of the table, listening and nodding after each suggestion.

At the end, I asked him what he thought. He told me that it was all good, but that he needed time to think about it. Now, my mandate was to get him to commit and sign a contract by the end of the day. I knew that if I left the business he would terrorize these employees, so I tried to move the conversation forward. Innocently, looking directly at him, man-to-man, I said, "Come on, Jim. Let's try some of these suggestions. What are you afraid of?"

That was the wrong question. Very wrong. He started to turn beet red, almost purple. A bystander would have sworn that I must have called his mother a *whore*. He was angry. He looked at me and said, "You try to railroad me in my own company? You piece of garbage. I'm going to kill you. I'm not afraid of anything."

He then stood up, grabbed a chair, and threw it at my head. He was a very strong guy. He was about 6'3" and lean. I never saw a man throw a boardroom chair that far and that accurately. It went across the room as if it were a baseball. Fortunately, I was still young and nimble, and the chair flew past me. My biggest problem then was that he stood between me and the exit door. The only way out was through him. I knew I could fight, but I was in a suit and tie, with slippery dress shoes. He was big, mean, and absolutely ready to beat me to a pulp.

Just as I mentally prepared myself for a few fists to the head, the other guys jumped in and held him back. It took all three of them to restrain him against a wall. At that moment, one of the guys said, "Get out of here, fast. Run!" So I quickly shuffled past them and out of the building. He continued to taunt and threaten me. He wasn't frothing at the mouth but spit accumulated around his lips and flopped around his chin as he yelled at me. He was absolutely unhinged.

To this day, I have never again asked someone, *"What are you afraid of?"*, nor do I put people on the spot like that in important meetings. When I know they are tense, and something is very uncomfortable, I have one-on-one meetings and I try to get them to vent before we get into a group setting. No one likes to be embarrassed or challenged in a group. If, at that time in Philadelphia, I had been more patient and mature, I would have been able to understand his real concerns. He still might have been an abusive, short-fused lunatic, but I might have been able to get through to him. I will never know. As it was, no one was helped in that situation.

After almost a year of working at a very intense pace, I felt it was time to leave. I also grew weary of the flexible morality in the company. The desire to grow quickly was also being fed with a permission to break rules. I didn't know what was actually being done; I just knew they were moving fast and cutting corners. I knew eventually it would catch up to them and I didn't want to be a part of it when it happened. Sure enough, a few years after I left the company, the lawsuits and criminal investigations piled up. Complaints to the Better Business Bureau mounted, and all credibility was diminished.

Again, I escaped unharmed, but I still hadn't learned my lesson from Moscow. Despite all of my self-proclamations to not be involved with troublemakers, I kept cutting the definitions of right and wrong too close; I believed that their work was not my work. I believed that if they were immoral or unjust, it was them acting improperly, not me. In this instance, I hadn't seen or heard of anything that was clearly criminal, so I thought it was okay, despite the fact that I felt that management was not proper.

It would take me a few more years to really learn the concept that a business is a living entity. Everyone that touches that business contributes to its life or its death. If it's rotten, and we know it and we do nothing to help change it, we're equally culpable in its demise and everyone it harms. As an analyst, I may not have crossed any lines of morality or criminality, but I certainly helped make the company a lot of money while I was employed there. That money helped them perpetuate their bad behavior on to others.

By the end of my tenure as a business analyst I felt that I now had a new toolkit that I could use in business. I felt like I had a lot more precision and technical knowledge about all aspects of a company. I now felt that I could buy and grow a business of my own. I wasn't really sure what kind of business I should buy, but I wanted to stay in the Midwest, closer to my friends and family. I thought that perhaps I should do something related to manufacturing because there was plenty of it in multiple industries within the region. It just seemed like the area with the most opportunities for improving and growing a business.

But then, one day, out of the blue, I received a fax from the Russian partner I had presumed dead. More than a year had passed, and we had not heard one word from him. According to his fax, he and his family were still alive, and he wanted to meet me in Baltimore in a couple of weeks. I thought that this was crazy, and I was afraid it could be a setup, but I also remembered what Russia was like. Crazy and unpredictable was the essential definition of Russia in those early years following the collapse of the Soviet Union. Anything was possible. So, I called the number and confirmed that it was actually him. He said he would explain everything in person.

Two weeks later, there he was, alive and looking just

like he did when I had seen him last: 6'1", broad shoulders, receding and thin black hair, pot belly, eyes drooping behind is owl-rimmed glasses. White dress shirt, black slacks, both properly pressed. He always looked sharp. His father had been a high-ranking Party member during the Soviet years, so he had learned to care about appearances.

He was in front of me, but I thought he was an apparition. It was a very strange phenomena to see him alive. It was confusing. My world and the story of my business in Russia ending made sense if he was dead, but he wasn't. How could he be alive and let more than a year pass before contacting us? And, why not contact our other partner in Moscow? Why contact me? By fax? Why Baltimore? All of it so very strange, but no stranger than anything in my past.

We met at a restaurant by the water where he ordered a massive dish of blue crabs and proceeded to tell me a tale straight out of a crime novel. It was so complicated that I took out a pen and paper to keep track of what he was telling me.

While we were still in Russia, as partners in a bank, he had secretly taken a partnership in another bank, borrowing money to finance it. He hid all of this from me and our other partner. In his mind, this was perfectly legitimate. He didn't stop to consider that it might influence our other three businesses.

Moscow being as corrupt as it was, trouble eventually surfaced at his new, secretive bank. The bank manager at his new bank began stealing money—a lot of money, and he eventually disappeared. He stole so much money that they were unable to repay the millions they had borrowed to finance the bank. So, my ex-partner came up with the great idea of selling our bank license without telling us, and he had lined up a buyer who was willing to pay $3 million. He figured I wasn't the killing type, and that his chances of cheating me were better than cheating the other guys he owed money. However, before he could conclude the sale of the bank license, the people he borrowed from showed up at his home with very large, very powerful guns. He wasn't there when it happened. When he returned home, he found it riddled with bullets. He got scared and left town with his family, neglecting to tell us what had happened. Of course, he still needed to sell the bank license, so telling us would complicate that. He instead decided to give the actual physical documentation for the license to a trusted cousin, someone none of us knew. The trusted cousin would then arrange the sale and arrange for the safe return for the family. Time passed but he received no word on any front. Eventually, the cousin told him to meet him in Greece, where he would hand over the money from the sale of the bank license and then he could return to Russia. In the meantime, he had his family hiding in Bulgaria.

When my partner showed up in Greece, he realized he had been set up and framed in some way because the police arrested him upon arrival at the meeting spot. The cousin never arrived, and his wife and kids didn't know of his whereabouts because he chose to hide this from them for their safety.

He told me that he had found God during his six months in a Greek jail. He learned that he had done many wrong things but now all was better because he was with God.

He then went on to explain that his very trusted cousin had betrayed him by taking the license to someone else who was going to pay him more money. Sadly, however, he too was betrayed. He was killed, and his body was found in a dumpster in Moscow.

I looked at my piece of paper, now full of names, places, circles, arrows, and dollar amounts, and I thought, *I lost everything because of this?* The explosives, the machine gunning, and the guys sitting outside of my house were all because of him—all because of greed. He wasn't happy enough with the success of our company; he decided to start another and hide it from us. Then when he got into trouble, he wanted to steal from us. Now, after telling me all of this, after confessing that our business was ruined by him and that our families and employees were almost killed because of him, he was now telling me that everything was better because he had found God. Really? Does God have my money? If so, I would like it back.

More than an hour had passed, and I hadn't even touched my food. I just stared at the piece of paper and thought about how dramatically my life had changed since I last saw him. I thought about the hundreds of nights in cheap motels, the lousy coffee and sleepless nights. How I'd been running ragged trying to learn how to properly work a financial calculator and run a business like an engineer. I was tired and now very angry. I had to uproot my life when I lost everything because of his greed. The level of betrayal and the chain of corruption and crime was staggering to me. However, in a way, it was a relief because it confirmed to me that doing business in Russia was unquestionably and consistently dangerous, and there was no way around it. Nevertheless, I was still angry.

I looked at him and said, "If you truly found God then you understand that you need to make amends for your sins. You owe me millions. When you pay it back all will be forgiven."

Humbly, he stared at me and said, "I know." We shook hands and I left.

I would never see him again, however. I received Christmas cards from him from time to time, but I have yet to receive one penny of the money he stole from me.

I resumed my search for a business to buy. I began by meeting with investment bankers and brokers. After months of meetings, no real prospects came to fruition. Then, one day, a friend suggested that I meet with a consultant who did a lot of work with small manufacturers. In this meeting I would hear the phrase "turnaround management" for the first time. I had no idea what it was.

I then came to learn of an entirely different category of business management. It appeared to be a commando style of management—a style designed for troubled and distressed businesses. This was a little-known world of restructurings and bankruptcies. Despite three years of law school, there was one course I never studied: bankruptcy. I knew nothing about this area of business, but I became intrigued. And despite spending a year immersed in practical MBA training, I had never heard the terms this guy was using. He showed me a couple of books that he had written— comprehensive texts on fixing troubled companies. He was very knowledgeable in turnaround work, but he had a significant problem in his own business: He didn't know how to grow his own revenue. After 10 years of existence, he had barely grown. He was impressed by my experience in growing my company in Russia and, in turn, I was impressed by his technical acumen.

We decided to strike a deal. I would help him grow his business and he would teach me more of the mechanics of analyzing and operating a business. My thought was that I would extend my practical MBA training. I planned to spend another year studying while being paid to work as a consultant and then I would go buy my own business.

However, once again life would not take a straight line. I didn't buy a business. Life moved very quickly and spectacularly. I was having fun so I didn't want to change environments. I spent the next five years at this firm learning and growing in more ways than I could have imagined.

In the beginning, my job was simple: selling. I made sales calls five to seven days per week, and I met with as many lawyers, bankers, investment bankers, accountants, consultants, and business owners as I could. I went up and down half of the country calling on everyone and attending any networking event that I found. As a former business owner, I viewed it as being paid to make friends. Within a couple of years, I had close to 2,000 new contacts in my personal database.

Many business owners discount or dislike the networking process. It takes a lot of time and there are never any guarantees with regard to whom you may or may not get business from. However, I viewed it as reconnaissance: go out, look and listen; ask lots of questions, and take notes. You will discover patterns of behavior and thinking that you can't read about. Every outing is an opportunity to learn about something new in the marketplace, and each person you meet is another potential avenue to future business. I have always generated revenue from the least likely of places simply because I was willing to make friends in the least likely of places.

As I made friends, our small firm of a few people grew. Within a couple of years, we had grown from a regional firm to working on national and international venues. As we grew, we continued to expand our sphere of learning and influence. By design, we tried to create an active learning environment. We were in the advice business, so we concluded that we had to continually study best management and operational practices. We shared articles and books with each other daily. We took courses on everything from industrial engineering to emotional intelligence. We tried to go beyond the traditional model of turnaround consulting. We wanted to step outside of the accounting and balance sheet restructuring practices and actually help redesign companies. A central theme to our turnaround plans was changing corporate culture by actively engaging employees. "Buy-in" was an important mantra. We knew that the best and fastest way to turn a company around was to get employees to buy into a turnaround process. The key to this philosophy was understanding that you don't get employees to buy in by dictating to them. You have to involve them in the process. In short, you tell them where you need to go and then ask them what needs to be done to get there. Most executives believe that they are steering a ship. In reality, it's the employees who are in control. The best answers to any problem are always on the front lines of any business.

In these early years at the turnaround firm, it was not uncommon for me to read one to three new books per week. Hundreds of business books are published every year, and I was determined to read as many as I could—everything from operations to marketing. I was searching for best practices in every field. When I wasn't reading, I was looking for seminars to attend.

I actively began learning more about human communication. I knew that people were highly stressed and fractured in many of my meetings, and I wanted to learn how to be a better communicator in these situations. I knew that if they didn't hear me, I stood no chance of saving the company. I also took courses with trial attorneys to learn how to effectively persuade juries. Like many things, it is part art and part science, but it's extremely valuable when you absolutely need to get your point across.

For several years, I put no limits on my learning. I read about extreme sports, shamans, and NASA, along with everything else. I was continually searching for ways to train myself to lead a business and help others in trouble.

Despite my personal learning quest and our firm's educational laboratory endeavors, we still couldn't escape the reality that we were dealing with severely distressed companies. The fringes of human frailty were important, but first and foremost we were dealing with business. We had to make the business profitable and make it pay its debts fast, or we had nothing.

What made it more challenging is that many of these clients had been great companies at some point in the past. They weren't just businesses; they had significant history. Most had been born, raised, and flourished during the decades of incredible growth in America. Occasionally, they were companies that were more than a hundred years old. They had lived through multiple wars, depression, recession, and great expansion. They were examples of survival, perseverance, and ingenuity. They had been shining and perfect examples of the American dream, but now they were examples of the harsh realities of life. All things come to an end, yet my colleagues and I thought that we could defy all the natural forces of decline and decay. We thought that we could extend life or even recreate it. To do this, we had to have the courage to walk right in the middle of all of the lost glory and immerse ourselves in the current, palpable pain.

I remember meeting this one particular client that was in a horrible situation. When I walked into his office, Mark, the owner, was sitting at his desk with his head down and his hands clenched. His office was filled with pictures of political luminaries from the past 40 years. He had sponsored and endorsed all levels of politics right up to presidential candidates. He had donated millions to their political coffers and had raised even more for them. I saw row after row of happy pictures, party pictures, and times of great celebration. But that seemed to be in the distant past.

I took a seat in front of him. He had a difficult time making eye contact and he said "hello" but nothing else. Now in his 70s, he appeared to be nothing like the man in the pictures; he was ashen and frail. I knew that I would have to carry the conversation.

"Mark, that's quite an impressive wall. Who was your favorite?" I asked.

There was a long pause. His hands stayed clenched as he lifted his head and said, "He inherited my disease. I tried to help him but there was nothing that I could do. Miserable disease."

Confused, I asked, "Who?"

Mark pointed over my shoulder. I turned to see a glass cabinet in the corner. Inside there was a folded-up American flag and a picture of a man in dress blues.

"My son," he replied.

I nodded and let the moment be.

"He suffered from depression like me. He fought it, but it got him. He killed himself just about a year ago. He used the rifle my father had given him as a teenager."

"I'm sorry, Mark. That's terrible."

"It *is* terrible. And I'm terrible. I knew, and I could have done something. I could have done more. I made all of the wrong decisions." Mark became angry. He clenched his hands tighter and began to shake. In an instant he pushed back his chair and stood up.

"Domenic, can I get you something to drink? How about a Diet Coke™?"

"Actually, I'm okay. But thanks," I replied.

He then walked across the room. It was a large office. In the distance, a light was on in what appeared to be a closet or pantry. Mark walked into it and I lost sight of him. Minutes passed, and I heard nothing. My mind raced as I wondered if he might be looking for a gun. He had just admitted to me that he suffered from depression and his son had committed suicide because of the same problem. It was not a big leap to think he might do the same at this very moment. This wasn't the first client that pulled out a gun in front me and threatened to kill himself. In those circumstances I was able to disarm them by asking them a simple question: "Okay, so you kill yourself. What happens next?" That question halted them and got them thinking about consequences.

However, this situation felt different. Mark was strung out and visibly shaking. I didn't know what he would do. It was possible that out of desperation, he would come out of that room with a gun and shoot me first. I was there because the bank had told him he had to speak with me. As far as he knew, I was a spy for the people that were about to close his business down. I debated leaving but I feared any sense of panic might further enrage him. So, I just sat there, praying for the best.

Three minutes later he reappeared, Diet Coke™ in hand.

The color had returned to his face. He sat down, smiled, and calmly asked, "So, the bank wants me to talk with you. What do you think you can do for us?"

In the next few hours I would learn of the dramatic rise and incredible fall of this 50-year-old company. Mark had come along at just the right time to be a commercial construction supplier. America had enjoyed a tremendous economic expansion since the '60s. In particular, Mark's company supplied materials for fast food restaurants. He was one of the top vendors to all of the best and fastest-growing food chains.

Mark had three sons, all of whom had worked in the business. Ten years earlier, Mark had received an offer to buy his business for $75M. It was the crowning moment of his storied entrepreneurial life. He would divide the proceeds into four equal amounts; one for him and his wife, and the other for his three boys. They would be financially set for their entire lives. But his boys saw it differently. They were in their early 40s; they were young and eager to recreate their father's path. They argued that if the company was worth $75M now that they could expand and make it worth $150M in 10 years or less. They were convinced that if they took their skills and diversified into the residential construction supply market that they could be just as successful as they were in the commercial market.

Mark decided to give them their chance. He didn't want to deny them the same opportunities that had been presented to him, so he turned down the offer to sell his company.

Ten years passed. The business was now deeply in debt and had lost 40% of its market share. The two remaining brothers had stopped speaking to each other.

Mark began to cry. "I knew that they couldn't do it. I knew

that they didn't have it in them. I knew it, but I didn't have the courage to say it out loud. I should have taken the money and gone on my way."

The three brothers had taken over principal operations 10 years earlier. They expanded into the residential market, building new plants, new distribution centers, and new offices in a different state. They also hired new staff at every level. On paper, it looked like it could be another great success. In reality, however, it was a managerial mess. They hired inadequately experienced production managers, quality control problems significantly hampered their ability to attract and keep customers, and weak sales and poor financial performance led to a revolving door of employees.

Years passed and revenues continued to drop as the boys tried to solve the problem. They threw more capital and more staff at the new division, both of which they had borrowed from the original company. With a thinned-out senior staff and a weakened balance sheet, the problems of the new company eventually entered the old company. The arguments increased, there was a daily slamming of phones and doors, and then, completely exasperated, one brother killed himself. Everyone stopped talking and the company came to a virtual standstill.

After a 30-year relationship, the bank was concerned about the future of Mark's company. They asked for an independent assessment of the situation.

As we dug into the company we confirmed that its expansion had been, in fact, a giant mistake. However, there were dozens of other smaller mistakes that had contributed to their downfall. The new market was a challenge, but there were countless opportunities to improve the quality and performance of the core business for each group. It had been a big stumble, but they had managed to create some value. This was still a viable company. With renewed focus and new procedures, it could be very successful again.

However, nothing could change unless change happened at the top. The two brothers, as owners, would have to be removed from their positions as president and COO. They were nice enough people, but they did not have the capacity or the respect from their employees to lead this company. They had some good thoughts and practices but not enough to be consistently successful. The message would have to come from the principal shareholder, their father.

I sat with Mark as he delivered the somber news to his boys. He gave one the option of working in sales and the other in accounting. He focused on the one reasonable skill that each had. The other option was that he would keep them on the payroll for one year as they tried to find work outside of the family business. They would still be owners, but they would have no managerial authority. They took the news as badly as expected but they had little choice; either leave or slide into eventual bankruptcy.

Mark stayed on as CEO. In the coming year we would implement a unified strategic vision and plan for the entire company. Many senior managers were replaced, and accountability was introduced at all levels. Production was updated with Kaizen and Six Sigma programs, and slow-moving products were shed. Quality improved as did financial performance. Previous customers gave us another chance, and new customers came into the fold.

Mark eventually retired, and we helped him recruit a new CEO from the outside. His two sons now sit on the board of directors and cash their annual dividend checks from the newly returned profits. It was a tremendous success and eternally satisfying. It was a powerful example of how you can repair almost anything with enough skill, determination, and cooperation.

Not long after this successful turnaround, I found myself in another multigenerational phenomena, stranger and even more poetic than I could even imagine. I refer to it as the "Tale of Two Georges"—George the First and George the Last. They were not related by blood and not related in character or disposition. The only thing they had in common was a 145-year-old company that had been started before the Civil War.

George the Last was a dispassionate, shrewd investor. Like all opportunists, he kept looking until he found the right deal, and he wound up buying a $75M shoe retailer with no money out of his pocket. It was the orphan of a huge, multinational conglomerate. Somehow, $75M in revenue was seen as insignificant so George cut a deal to where he would pay nothing for it; he would simply assume the debt and take over this company. He put in place a lender and then started his reign.

George the Last did what so many heartless, cold investors do—he systemically cut out expenses and took all of the cash out of the business for himself. It was all profit; the faster the better. Within the first year, he had closed 40 of the 100 retail locations and fired 90% of the corporate staff. At this point, having taken out tens of millions for himself, he planned to sell the business for an even greater profit. He figured he had right-sized the business. But George the Last wasn't a leader, business manager, or entrepreneur. He didn't know how to grow things; he only knew how to pillage and kill for profit. This time, he had gone too far. He cut too deeply, left the company with no cash, and the company began to implode. Some stores sales were decreasing by double digits, margins were collapsing, and there was no plan to turn the company around. George the Last had made millions buying this company with no cash outlay but he had made one very big and very crucial mistake; he signed a personal guarantee for the company's debt. It was a critical mistake for an otherwise perfect, heartless scumbag. The company had a $10M credit line and George needed a plan to get his name off of it before the company filed for bankruptcy. So that was my contract: to get George the Last out of the personal guarantee.

I explained to him that the only way to do that was to fix the company, then refinance it on its own merits. However, this would take time. It also would take money, but he refused to invest one penny. He had to stay true to his corporate raping and pillaging ways. He hired us on a very limited engagement and a small budget to conduct an assessment, but before he moved forward, he wanted a guaranteed plan that it would work.

Despite being seasoned retail and shoe industry professionals, not one executive in the company believed that it could be fixed. Similarly, not one of my colleagues, established turnaround experts, believed that it could be fixed. Lenders and investment bankers did not believe it either. Everyone thought that it was dead. However, I wasn't convinced. I decided to ask a different question: "Why is it still alive?" I wondered how it was still standing, through all of the abuse and extreme cuts, what kept it moving forward? There had to be something keeping it afloat.

I also looked at the company's storied history. It was approaching 145 years in existence. At one time, it was the largest shoe manufacturer and retailer in the country; at its peak it had more than 600 retail locations across the nation. It was a true, American, industrial success. I thought that because of its history, that alone was reason to try to save it.

One of its principal leaders and owners in the 20th century was a benevolent and fabulous thinker. He was George the First. Unlike other industrialists of the time that paid workers a flat fee (like Ford Motor Co., which paid a record-setting amount of $5 a day), he believed people needed something to look forward to each day. He believed people should be paid for their performance—for what they produced.

George the First was a true pioneer of "corporate welfare." He believed that companies should take care of their employees; not to coddle them, but to help them be part of a community as well as a workforce. He had company grocery stores where he sold produce from their fields at cost to employees. He had a home-building program through which employees could buy homes at cost and get them financed through the company. He also designed and built a golf course for employees that had no sand traps or hills. When they asked why he did this, he said, "A man works hard enough all day. He doesn't need those extra challenges on the course." His CFO came to him one day and said, "People keep taking the wheelbarrows at the job sites for the homes. We have to do something about it." He responded by saying, "Just keep buying wheelbarrows. Eventually everyone will have one and we won't have to worry about it." This man, George the First, was a man of great heart, vision, and management style and a tremendous humanitarian. Certainly, there had to be a way to save this company and this legacy.

I had five weeks to conduct an assessment and come up with a turnaround plan. We were officially hired during the last week of November, and on January 2 I was to deliver my findings. With a short schedule and the holidays, I decided to leave the board room and all of the naysayers. I wanted to try to look at the company with fresh eyes, as a blank slate, so I decided to visit a third of the retail locations anonymously. I wanted to experience shopping as a customer off the street. I would also visit some stores with notice, letting them know who I was, so I was able to ask questions in greater detail. I also spoke with the beleaguered remaining staff at corporate headquarters. After two weeks of travel and interviews I found something that was not being reflected in financial statements or in the boardroom. I found the reason this company was still alive. I found heart and intellect among the employees.

There were hundreds of caring and intelligent employees. In the past 50 years, since the death of the benevolent leader, the company had been sold and resold to big, multinational companies. Every time it changed ownership, they changed strategies and management practices. By the time I was hired, it was a company that didn't know what it was. It had six "core customer groups;" It was urban, rural, young, old, male, and female. And, after 18 months with George the Last, it was skinny, starving, and shaking in the freezing cold.

The turnover at the managerial level was 80% while the turnover at the sales associate level was close to 90%. New employees left as fast as they were hired. People were miserable and frustrated, but there was a small, core group of "lifetime" employees who cared and were very knowledgeable. Management had ignored them for years. I listened to them and I took notes.

I had evaluated retail companies in the past but nothing this large or diverse. After reviewing all of the internal notes,

I decided to research best practices within the retail industry, so I went to one of my favorite spots for answers: the library. Over the course of a week, I poured through dozens of books and took all of the best ideas. In drafting my assessment and proposed turnaround plan, I combined many of the employee suggestions with my own thoughts on best retail practices, and all of this had to be done with practically zero additional cash. Every penny was desperately needed for existing operations.

I finished preparing the presentation on January 1, ready to be delivered the next day. George the Last sat at the head of the table, flanked by all of his executives. Patiently, page by page, I showed him that we could turn this company around in six to nine months, with no additional capital from him. At that point we could try to refinance him out from the personal guarantee. It was crisp, simple, and straightforward.

The room fell silent and each executive sat expressionless. Suddenly, the CEO looked at George and said, "It will never work. This is utter garbage." George looked around the table at the still expressionless executives, then looked at me and nodded in approval. At that moment, the industry veteran, the highly paid corporate whore of a CEO who had helped rape and pillage and take bonuses, stood up and said, "It's either him or me." Without missing a beat, George the Last said to him, "You're fired." The CEO stormed out of the room, never to be seen again. Then George turned to me and said, "Okay, kid, you're up. You're the CEO."

Typically, someone would be very excited at such recognition and a promotion. But I was 32 years old. I had never run a company this big, and I knew very little about the shoe or retail industry other than what I had read two weeks earlier. I wanted to be a leader, but in this situation, I just saw myself as an analyst. I was sitting in a room filled with six people who all had a minimum of 20 years of industry experience. I didn't think that I was ready for this role, but, for some reason, I didn't say "no." After my moment of doubt and panic, I smiled and said, "Okay. Let's get to work."

Within a few days of being appointed the CEO, I would be presented with another personal touch of history to this company. In speaking with my mother, I learned that my grandfather's brother had worked at this company when he emigrated from Italy. He spent 20 years working in the manufacturing facilities, toiling and sweating over leather and dyes with thousands of other workers. It was a surreal moment for me. Out of the blue, this opportunity was presented to me—a century-old company in a small town that employed my great uncle, and now I was responsible for saving it. My family went from the fields to the front office in a short amount of time. For me, it now added another layer of pride and responsibility. I didn't need the extra motivation, but now I had it.

I got to work on the turnaround plan quickly. We implemented every one of the line-item suggestions within a couple of weeks. We narrowed the product focus, brought in high-margin, high-turning products, got closer to our loyal customers, and put in place true sales training and a better incentive program for sales associates. We had internal sales contests for daily and weekly bonuses. I made certain that the money was delivered each day to keep motivation high. Cash in hand never fails. We had potluck lunches and pizza parties. I opened all of the books for all of the managers across the country, and I showed them exactly what we did and did not have. We didn't have money for a new point-of-sale system or new computers. So, in their place, we would have to gather data the old-fashioned way; with pen and paper. Every day, sheets of sales statistics were faxed to me from all 40 locations. Very quickly we gained clarity over the company and the strategic direction. As this happened, employees became reinvigorated and focused. Most of all, we tried to have as much fun as we could. Laughter was as important as goals.

Within a few months, the company started to turn. The efforts were showing up on the financial statements, and employee turnover had been reduced to almost zero. No one was leaving; they liked working for us. Margins improved, and inventory turns improved. Sales decline stopped and went upwards—customers liked us again. All of this happened with no new technology, no money for store renovations, and no money for advertising or brand marketing. We did it with focus on productivity, profitability, and most importantly on the customer. We brought heart and intellect back to the company.

At the seventh month, progress was positive enough to go to market for a new lender. We would show the ugly past and illustrate, line by line, how we had turned and continued to turn the company around. Banks were impressed. We received several offers to refinance the debt. Within 60 days we were able to get George the Last a new lender, and with this new lender also came a release from his personal guarantee. The bank deemed the company healthy enough to be financed on its own. It was a great success for everyone.

However, I wish the Tale of the Two Georges would have ended there, but it didn't. The company had changed but George the Last had not. He was still the heartless, shrewd investor. He still owned the company and I was just the hired help. He thanked me for my efforts; my contract was complete. Within a month, I was replaced with a hatchet man. George, now free of his personal guarantee of the debt, could resume chopping this company down and sucking out all of the cash we had worked so hard to restore.

When I heard what was happening, I tried to persuade George to sell the company. I tried to find buyers, but I was unable to do so. Most feared that irreparable damage was already being done. I tried to organize an employee buyout, but I couldn't get there. Not enough of them had the ability to make the investment. I tried to open doors, but it seemed that all my luck had been used up. It just seemed like there was nothing else I could do.

Over the next 12 months, the company would be liquidated, and all employees were let go. Its logo and brands were sold or shuttered. After 146 years of surviving in the business world it had come to a bitter, cold end. George the First would succumb to George the Last.

This event—this calculated, cold closing of a profitable, well managed, storied company—left me frustrated and bitter. Again, I had built up a business, worked hard, and thrived and, once again, a thug was taking it away from me. In Russia, there were gangsters; I understood that. But now I was in America. These things were not supposed to happen. I thought it was just about profit and loss. This company was profitable, so it should live. Apparently, for George, it was too much trouble. In the three years he owned the company, he visited the corporate headquarters once and never once visited any of the retail locations. He managed all of his destruction at the foot of his grotesquely overpriced desk, far, far away. For all that I had studied about best practices and the nuances of the human psyche in trauma, I forgot to calculate the stupidity of people with power. It was his company; he could kill it if he wanted to.

The irony of all of this is that a great deal of accolades came my way after the turn of this company. As I shopped around for new lenders, they could see my work over the past year. Apparently, turning a retailer around with no money is very difficult. Word spread, and I now had significant credibility in more financial circles.

One day, my firm received a call from a small retail consulting business. No one had ever heard of them, but they had heard of us, and they asked for a meeting on a retail company they were advising. They wouldn't tell us the name of their client, but they did tell us that it did $3 billion in sales. That was a revenue far greater than we had ever worked with in the past. Prior to that point, I believe the largest client had $200 million in sales. I found all of this amusing and surreal; I didn't actually believe that it was true. After turning the shoe company around, I was now the firm's retail specialist, so I was tasked with attending this meeting. I gathered the partners' names and did research on them. It turned out that this small consulting firm had once helped build the largest retailer in the world: Walmart™.

A handful of senior executives who were key to building Walmart™ with Sam Walton had retired and set up a consulting firm. They were very rich but very bored, so they decided to keep working. Part of this group included the former head of International Sales, Logistics, Merchandising, and Operations. These were heavyweights in the corporate world with extremely impressive credentials. I had absolutely no idea why they wanted to talk with me.

I flew to Maryland and met them at their preferred location: Olive Garden. When I arrived, they were all already there, sitting happily with glasses of bourbon and dishes of fettucine Alfredo. Apparently they were hungry so they started without me.

They were very welcoming and very professional. Each had a small notepad and pen by the right side of the pasta. They went around the table, introduced themselves, and stated a brief bio. It was a recital of giant proportions: *President of this, president of that, oversaw $100 billion in revenue, managed 5,000 locations and 300,000 employees.* The sheer numbers behind each of their jobs were staggering. They were almost incomprehensible to someone like me who had only managed a few hundred employees. By the time they got to me, I couldn't wipe the smile off my face. I still could not understand what I could possibly teach them, so I asked.

In short, the answer was, "Domenic, we know how to work with money. We've always had a barrel full of it. When we needed to do something, we just went to the barrel. But now we're working with companies that don't have a dollar to spare. They tell us that you know how to fix companies without any money. We're hoping you could teach us how to do that."

Imagine that? A little mouse was going to teach an elephant a new dance. It is proof positive that there is a place for everyone in the business world if you can add value to someone else's life.

What I admired most about this situation was that these very intelligent, very accomplished, and very wealthy men were still willing to learn. They had open minds and were still curious and excited about business. That was admirable.

They continued to eat and drink as I began sharing a few thoughts on distressed retailers. Every time I mentioned something new, at least half of them put down their forks and took diligent notes. I was supposed to be teaching, but I learned far more from them. It was a fascinating lesson in leadership for me. Always be willing to learn something new.

In the next couple of months we went on to form a joint-venture partnership between our two firms. We actively marketed our combined skills for distressed and retail services. Over the following year, as we spent time together, I learned some of the clever but harsh secrets of Walmart™'s success.

Walmart™ literally changed the landscape of many businesses across America. They changed the way in which consumers shopped but they also changed the dynamic between retailer and supplier. They took very aggressive positions with suppliers, most of them manufacturers. For example, when a manufacturer won a contract with Walmart™, Walmart™ would expect delivery in 30 days, but they would pay the supplier in 90 days. Typically, a new supplier to Walmart™ would immediately have to extend their own company's line of credit when they secured a signed purchase order. In some cases, the initial orders were so large, suppliers would buy new machinery, hire more employees, and even build new facilities to accommodate the size of the production. Banks were more than willing to help them with all of this. They extended credit freely. Everyone felt comfortably secured doing business with the largest retailer in the world. That first contract always felt like they had just won the lotto.

With credit line in place, manufacturing would begin and then the supplier would ship product on time—no one wanted to be late for Walmart™. Their product would arrive on time and then be promptly put on the shelves within the stores. If it sold well, Walmart™ still didn't pay early. They would hold on to the supplier's money for as long as possible. If it didn't sell well or sales started to slow, they would call the supplier and tell them that they were lowering the sales price, and they were going to reflect that reduction in their original purchase price. Even though they had previously agreed to a specific price and the supplier built the product to that price, Walmart™ would unilaterally renegotiate a deal whenever they wanted. No one ever argued. Why? Because they still hadn't received a dime from Walmart™. They had borrowed from the bank to accommodate the large production order, and now they didn't want to make waves for fear of being caught in litigation with a giant company that certainly had great lawyers. If they complained, it could take years to see any payment. In the meantime, they might have to close their own business because the friendly banker absolutely expected payment on the credit line. If you supplied Walmart™, you towed the line, regardless of the demands.

This pattern of behavior continued. It didn't just stop at one price reduction for your product. Walmart™ kept lowering the price until it sold. Everyone remembers their advertisements and commercials: "Catch the Falling Prices." It was great for them and for the consumer, but it was terrible for the manufacturer.

If, after all of the price reductions, any product still remained, they would send it back to the supplier and they would charge them for the shipping. At this point, the supplier had no choice but to comply because they had to pay off their debt, so they took whatever money they could get. Then they hoped they could get another contract with Walmart™ to make up the shortfall on the first order. Unless the product was a total dud, Walmart™ would give them another chance—because in the end, it really wasn't costing them anything. Essentially, they were a consignment shop; suppliers sent their products to Walmart™ and if they sold, they took a percentage. If they didn't sell, all of the burden was on the supplier. They could argue that they had lost the opportunity to sell something more profitable, which is true. In the end, however, they never lost. They became a giant not because of their retailing experience but because they understood finance better than their competitors.

Not only would they minimize their risk on purchasing products, but they would use the excess cash to invest in other financial instruments. They had the supplier's product and they would collect payment from customers immediately, but they still had 90 days to pay the supplier. That gave them plenty of time and cash to put into the public markets, bonds, etc. They were always a cash-rich company because they used their suppliers as their lender, interest free.

This approach to retailing was very aggressive, but I learned from these senior executives that they took this supplier-based financing model one step further. Something unimaginable to most.

When Walmart™ designated a new store location for construction, they would visit an existing supplier and get him very excited with the prospect of additional revenue. They eagerly presented him with big numbers for future orders. Concurrently, they showed him the blueprints for the new store. They would razzle and dazzle about how beautiful and state-of-the-art the new location would be. Then they would show him on the blueprints where his product would be specifically featured within the store. It was all very grandiose and filled with promise. Everyone would smile and dream a little. Finally, at that very moment when the supplier was gleeful and counting his new fortunes, Walmart™ executives would hand him an invoice. The supplier, confused, would look at the invoice and ask, "What's this?" The Walmart™ executives would then explain that the invoice was the estimated construction cost for that particular space within the store. It included everything from cement to electricity. Then they would smile and deliver the message: "You can either pay this or your space in the shiny new store will go to your competitor." Was this nasty? Or clever? You tell me.

Historically, retailers would ask suppliers to share costs for advertising or special promotions. This evolved to "slotting fees"—paying a price for premium shelving. Then, along came Walmart™, which took it so far down the road that it changed retailing forever. They proudly bragged about having new stores entirely paid for before the first shovel hit the ground.

They made their shareholders a tremendous amount of money, and they delivered exactly what the customer wanted—cheaper prices. But from my perspective, it was difficult to hear. Prior to meeting them, I spent several years working across America's traditional manufacturing zones. Industry after industry, client after client, they were suffering and ultimately closing their factories because operations were being moved overseas in search of cheaper costs to accommodate retailers. Many of them had the same story: their downfall started the moment they signed a big contract with Walmart™. Some would say Home Depot™ or Lowe's™, since they too would eventually adopt these aggressive purchasing practices.

My new partners always treated me with kindness and

the utmost respect. I admired their success, but I don't know if I would have done what they did. They freely leveraged power to intimidate—not dissimilar to the mafia. It was often just a shakedown for more money. However, to be fair, every supplier knew how aggressive Walmart™ could be. They were always polite but they were never shy. You knew that upfront. Suppliers took the risk, so they shared in the responsibility for their own demise.

Somewhere in the middle of my new venture with the Walmart™ executives, I was invited to participate in an even more extraordinary partnership. My name and reputation were finding themselves into different circles, and somehow it found its way to high levels of the Chinese government.

It was at this point when I was asked to be an operational advisor for the Economic Development Ministers of Shanghai and Nanchang. The Chinese government wanted help for all of their state-owned enterprises, so they turned to countless executives from the Western world for help in transitioning from a Communist model of operations in business to a capitalist model.

This was a very exciting opportunity. China was still in the early stages of developing what would eventually become a powerhouse economy. Similar to Russia, it was a unique moment in time and I wanted to be a part of it. I quickly agreed to work with them, and within a week they would deliver a stack of dozens of companies for me to analyze. Actually, they asked to skip the analysis and just said, "Choose which company you would like to run. We can offer you a very generous contract." I was honored, but I had never been to China, nor did I know much about the culture. I thought, at a minimum, I should visit before committing to a long-term consulting contract. I agreed to meet them in China and analyze approximately 10 companies.

My meetings were with very large companies that employed anywhere from 5,000 to 35,000 employees. Under the communist model, state-owned employers were required to provide virtually all social and welfare services to their employees. Each business was essentially a city unto itself. They had schools, grocery stores, hospitals, and residences—thousands of apartments for all of the employees and their families. The challenge for all of these companies was that the government was now asking them to be profitable (like a capitalist company) but they still had to provide all of these services for the employees (like a communist company).

I met with the senior executives of companies in several different industries, most notably paper, steel, pharmaceutical, and light manufacturing. All of the CEOs were under a great deal of pressure with this change in business model. Profitability was not a primary issue in the past; however, now it was front and center. They struggled with the competing dynamics of being profitable but still providing for the entire community. To be profitable, in some cases, they would have to lay off thousands of employees. However, as part of their duty to the state, they still had to pay for their housing, medicine, education, etc.

Furthermore, they wondered what all of these thousands of people would do all day long if they didn't have a job. Their homes were within the company compound. Would the unemployed live with terrible shame? What other options did they have? Where would they go without any money? It was a tremendous burden, an almost impossible situation for the leaders of companies. I now understood why they were actively looking for new leaders—no one wanted to do the "dirty" work of firing but still providing for thousands of people and their families. As I visited in each company, I offered suggestions on how they could improve operations, but I had no good answers to this larger social responsibility.

While in China, I spent a great deal of time asking them about their history and their way of life. I also actively read several books trying to better understand the Chinese culture and their approach to business. If I was going to help them, I needed to understand where they came from and what mattered most to them. Through conversation and my textbooks, I learned that there were driving principles that could be found in Confucianism and in the book *Thick Face, Black Heart* that were important to understanding the Chinese business environment. It was a complex culture. Not everything could be understood in straight lines. For example, it takes a long time to get to know what is actually being represented in a place of work. You never knew if you were being told the truth or being told what they thought you wanted to hear. Why didn't they tell the truth? Because it might embarrass someone, including you. This type of thinking made it very challenging to solve problems in the workplace. You could sit at a table filled with managers and no one would tell you exactly how they felt or the real source of the problem. In their world, it was more respectful to stay silent.

My task was to help them become more capitalist in business. I could help them with operational changes, but cultural changes would be very difficult. I knew that if there were going to be changes in their behaviors and belief systems that it would take decades to manifest. This was not the type of phenomena that could be changed in isolation.

The greater community would have to slowly adjust to new habits and new processes. All of that would take a long time. I really liked the challenge of trying to help them through this difficult period of transition. It was an exciting proposition and a dynamic time in China, but I wasn't ready for a long-term commitment to live there. I enjoyed meeting people. I was treated exceptionally well. I was fascinated by the changes happening in their country, but I didn't think I was prepared to give up my life in America. When I left, I wished them well. Time would prove that they adapted just fine. China will soon be the biggest economy in the world.

At this point, life was great. My firm continued to grow and the projects we worked on continued to have many positive results. I grew as a professional and my credibility continued to rise. I had become a partner in our firm. All was moving smoothly and in the right direction.

The blessings and good fortune continued.

One day, I received an invitation from Harvard Business School. They were holding their very first turnaround symposium. They were only inviting a dozen turnaround specialists from around the country and I was on that short list. For many, this offer may have been a good honor—maybe even a *great* honor. For me, it was something unimaginable. I was the son of poor immigrants, I never went to business school, I had an Arts and Law degree, and now, in the matter of a couple years, I had partnered with Walmart™ executives and served as a business advisor to the Chinese government, and I was being asked to speak at the pre-eminent business school in the world. In 10 years, I went from not knowing that there was a difference between checking and savings accounts to speaking at Harvard Business School. What a fantastic life.

When the day of the symposium came, it was everything that I could imagine. A couple hundred students gathered to learn about crisis management, distressed investing, and turnaround consulting. At this time, in 2002, this was new and novel for Harvard. They were the first of the Ivy League business schools to be organizing such an event. There were no programs that taught this type of work. There may have been professors who occasionally used a case study about the turnaround of an underperforming company, but nothing like this. Nothing this comprehensive. This was a very different approach for a business school. Typically, the Ivy Leagues didn't prepare their students to work with companies that were out of cash. Harvard and the other top schools groomed their students to work with rich folks, on Wall Street, with the best banks and companies in the world. But in typical Harvard fashion, they were further down the road, exploring new ground.

I was impressed by both the caliber of questions from the students and the people presenting at the symposium. I was by far the youngest and least experienced of the group. The other speakers had far more capital and many more businesses under management than I had, but I still I was well received by the students. Turns out I had something the others didn't have—I had started an international company in my early 20s with no money. The students, being young and often in debt with school loans, wanted to know how I'd done it. They loved the fact that I knew nothing about business but still went for it. They liked the conversation so much that by the end of the day, I was given another offer; I was asked to visit the MIT Sloan School of Management to speak to their business class on my own. Again, it was a tremendous honor and very humbling.

As I flew home from Boston, I reflected on my journey up to this point. I thought about the mafia, coup attempts, death threats, losing my business, and then starting over from the bottom; all of the travel, the fleabag motels, the incessant reading, and the years of studying. I thought about rising again and saving a 145-year-old company, only to experience another brutal, cold loss. It was frustrating, but it helped me grow and mature.

I had come very far from my naïve early days. I was smarter, more accomplished, and surrounded by some of the brightest minds in business. I reflected on all of these events as I looked at my commemorative plaque from Harvard and thought, "Okay, I did it. I'm finally here. MIT is next. It's all good. The worst is behind me."

If only life was that simple.

Lessons for Life

1. Seek out mastery.

If you're going to pursue something, pursue it greatly. Master every aspect of your product or service. Don't just benchmark against any competitor; find the best in your field and other fields.

Task: Decide what you want to emulate or beat and then work toward it every day. You don't need to be great at everything; just masterful in the things customers are willing to pay you for.

Lessons for Life

2. Separate fact from opinion.

Everyone has an opinion, in good times and bad. Everyone will offer a point of view as to why you won or why you lost; they will present it as "facts." In business, the facts are on the page—they present themselves as numbers. Interpretation of those numbers is opinion.

Task: Challenge every conversation, every meeting, and every email in order to separate fact vs. opinion. It's perfectly acceptable to have opinions, but have the entire company get in the practice of dividing them from facts.

Lessons for Life

3. Dream about the future but work in the short-term.

Mission statements are nice, but they are best saved for the poetic thoughts of a bar or bedroom. Drive business plans on a daily, weekly, and, at most, monthly basis. If you have the stomach for it, drive them by the hour. Set hourly goals for your employees and see how rapidly your business and profits grow.

Task: Deconstruct your mission statement into tangible and measurable weekly and daily goals for each department and each person. Begin by measuring your actual performance against those goals on a weekly basis, then graduate to doing so daily. You should be able to capture all of these data points on a one-page Flash Report. Each critical driver of productivity and profitability should be on that page. This will allow you to capitalize on strengths and address weaknesses in a very timely manner.

Lessons for Life

4. Forget your gut; use your brain.

"Just a gut feeling" is often a justification for important decisions. The only thing your gut is telling you is that your past experiences are either affirming or rejecting the decision. You are either supportive of the direction or fearful of it based on nothing more than your past experiences. Winning is a habit; unfortunately, so is losing. There are countless bad decisions made by leaders who use the phrase "gut feeling." Seek out facts and hard data.

Task: Each time you are faced with an issue, either a problem or an opportunity, and you find yourself "just" deciding, ask yourself: "What is the basis for my decision?" If you don't have a concrete factual answer, ask the same question again. If the answer is, "It just feels right to me," keep digging because it's most likely similar to something you've experienced in the past. It's not some mystery psychic influence. Decide what is most important for your decision— past outcome or new path. If you need a new path, you need facts. Seek them out.

Lessons for Life

5. Determine value and non-value added.

"Value" is defined by the customer; it is the aspects that the customer pays for. Everything else is "non-value added." For example, a can of Coke™—the only value in a can of Coke™ is the brown, sugary water. Everything else is not of value to the customer. How the can is made, where it's made, how it's shipped, stored, and sold is irrelevant to the customer. They just want the same, tasty, brown, sugary water. Every business has to define value and non-value for itself. Once you determine this, work hard at minimizing or eliminating all non-value-added activities.

Task: Go through the supply chain of your business looking at each critical step in making a product or delivering a service. Involve all team members. At each step ask, "Why do we do this?" Ask it five times. Try to get to the base of understanding precisely what is valued by the customer. Whatever is not valued should be eliminated or minimized immediately.

Lessons for Life

6. In business, money is love.

How do you know your customers love you? They give you money. More money equals more love. There is no ambiguity. Make them love you and they will shower you with money.

Task: Ask your employees what products or services they "love." Find out what they love about them. Make a long list and then compare it to your own company. Go to your best customers and ask them what they love about your product or services. Ask them what they would "love" to see next. Find the love; make it grow. Minimize or throw out everything else.

Lessons for Life

7. Employees are not family.

You can't fire family, and most families are dysfunctional. Business demands clarity and efficiency; group hugs should be saved for holidays and funerals. Hire only the best. Define their role, goals, and mutually agreed upon expectations and review them every three months. If they can't achieve expectations in two consecutive quarters, fire them.

Task: If you are in a family business, develop a clear job description for each family member, including yourself. Define the goals and expectations for each position and measure them quarterly. When there are problems, put in place a plan to remedy them immediately. If you can't remedy the problems as a family, agree in advance that an independent third-party mediator will be brought in to help you clear the air and the logjam. You and everyone in the family has to be held to the same high standard as every employee.

If you're not in a family business but you've created an environment that routinely uses the term "We're a family," then you need to go through the same exercise. Longtime employees, friends, buddies, and nice folk all fall into the same category. Clarity and accountability yield the best for the most.

Lessons for Life

8. You can't manage what you can't measure.

If you measure it, you can find a way to improve it. Determine what drives (a) productivity and (b) profitability and tie it to what your customer values most. Then measure it often.

Task: Determine what drives productivity and profitability throughout the entire company. You are looking for specific tasks and items that contribute to efficiency (e.g., shortening the amount of time to make and deliver a product) and profitability (e.g., minimizing the amount of scrap material produced). Put all of them on one Flash Report. Typically, it shouldn't take up more than one page. You are looking exclusively for the key markers (not every marker). Once you've determined that it is an accurate steering panel then distribute it daily or weekly to everyone. Ask everyone, section by section, driver by driver, what can be done to improve that specific number. That relentless, timely focus will drive you further than any gut feeling or group hug.

Lessons for Life

9. What gets paid gets done.

If you want something done, tie an employee's compensation to it. Then you'll never have to debate or discuss it again.

Task: Determine what customers value most. Then determine what drives productivity and profitability to create that value. Once you know these goals, tie employees' compensation to achieving these goals. Every employee in the entire company should have their compensation tied to quantitative and qualitative goals. Every quarter or, at a minimum, biannually, there should be a review of these goals. It doesn't need to be long or complicated. It just needs to be of value to the customer, to productivity, and to profitability.

Lessons for Life

10. Be careful of the Three Wise Men.

Don't let your accountant, lawyer, and banker run your business. Every troubled business has weak advisors. Sometimes they are weak because they just don't have enough experience. Always try to find the best and the brightest in each field and make sure they stick to giving you advice only in their area of expertise.

Understand, accountants, lawyers, and bankers often think they are businessmen—but they're not. Your accountant is there to principally help you with tax matters—that's it. Accountants generally are not great at finance; finance is about predicting the business's financial needs, while accounting is about tallying about the past flows of the business. It's about what happened last month or last quarter. Your lawyer is there to give you legal advice—that's it. Run fast from a lawyer who starts telling you which markets you should enter and exit. Too often, particularly with more senior attorneys, they feel that they are "businessmen" because they've drafted so many legal documents—but they're not. They're not managing the business, day in and day out, dealing with countless issues that arise. They sit an office, reviewing contracts that were drafted by their juniors. Finally, with regard to your banker, it's the same as above. Your banker is there to sell you money—that's it. You borrow from them, they make a profit from you, and the relationship should end there. Of course, you want to make them feel comfortable about your business so you should provide them with a lot of detail. Why? Because the more certain they are, the more they will lend you, if you need it.

Task: Review clear goals and expectations for each Wise Man/Woman. Keep each one of them in their own lane. They can have group meetings but all of them should understand their place in the stakeholder group.

ADVERSITY

As business men and women, as leaders and entrepreneurs, our personal lives are brought to our workplace in many different ways. The challenges we face are not just technical in nature. As hard as some of us try, we can't keep everything in separate and neat little boxes. Often, these challenges spill over. Personal adversity then becomes business adversity. Sometimes there is no way to distinguish the two, but you still need to find a way to lead because people are depending on you.

After my experience in Russia, I vowed to never be deceived again. I had worked hard to study business and people to get close to them and understand every nuance. I put down the books on affirmations and I read books on handwriting analysis, facial examination, and forensic accounting. I studied liars, cheats, and experts in fraud. I wanted to see them coming. I wanted to be prepared.

At this point in my life, at 35, I was glib about nothing. I was focused. I thought that I was doing all of the right things personally and professionally. I worked hard, I exercised daily, and I ate the right foods. I drove a safe car. I donated money to good causes. I had a beautiful and loving wife and great friends—hundreds of friends. I had a great company. Overall, life was fantastic; I didn't think that it could get any better. Unfortunately, those feelings would be short-lived. The moment I thought that I was on top again was the very moment I was pushed off another mountain. The fall this time would be uglier, longer, and more painful.

Within a couple of weeks of speaking at Harvard, I would learn that my wife's struggle with mental illness was worse than I could have imagined. She had two dominating problems: acute bulimia and a genetic pre-disposition to schizophrenia. She had struggled with bulimia since we first met as teenagers. We dated briefly as teens, but the struggle was too much for her to hide from a boyfriend, so she broke up with me. When we reconnected four years later, she appeared to have put her problems behind her. We resumed dating and soon after, her struggle with bulimia and anorexia returned. As with many ailments, there are varying degrees. She would be categorized as "acute." At her worst, by her own admission, she would vomit 15 to 20 times a day.

Despite the severity of the problem, I thought it was surmountable. I was an eternal optimist. I would shower her with books and tapes on positive reinforcement, affirmations, and re-framing. It was a sea of people like Wayne Dyer, Deepak Chopra, Gary Zukav, and Marianne Williamson. I tried everything. Doctors, therapists, coaching, seminars with Anthony Robbins, but little of it stuck. She continued to struggle. I knew it was a serious issue. I knew it could have implications on our marriage and prospects for a family, but I believed that all of us have an issue to deal with and this was just hers. I thought to myself, *So what if she has a couple problems? All of us have problems, including me.*

When she was a teenager, those close to her knew of her struggle. However, now older, most thought she had overcome them. She hadn't but I decided to keep her secret from friends, family, and coworkers. I wanted her to have the dignity and privacy to deal with this on her own terms. At times, it was very difficult. Her electrolytes were often imbalanced, so she would routinely pass out. I'd find her on the bathroom floor or closet and bring her back to bed until she was better. For years I called doctors looking for advice and direction. I tried to get her to go for longer-term stays at clinics that specialized in eating disorders, but she wouldn't go.

Time marched on and her demeanor began to darken. She appeared to be displaying early symptoms of schizophrenia. This disease ran through one side of her family. Meanwhile, almost two decades of bulimia were causing her physical damage. The enamel on her teeth had worn out and they needed to be capped. She developed a heart murmur that seemed permanent. All of these issues weighed heavily on me. I worried every day that she might have a heart attack and that there was greater permanent internal damage on other organs. And now I worried that if indeed she had schizophrenia, her world would close in further.

Then, one day, in a letter to me, she confided that she had been lying about her whereabouts every day for more than a year. Almost every day, she would call me and tell me she was working late. How late? "Not sure" was always the answer. I told her it was fine and to take her time. I would make dinner and wait for her. On most nights she would show up at eight, sometimes nine. I was there, dinner table set, waiting patiently. I thought it was great; I admired her work ethic. I worked hard, and she was always supportive, so I returned the respect and support. I thought this is what you're supposed to do in a relationship. But now, in this letter, I was reading about not just one lie but *hundreds* of lies.

At this point we had been friends for more than 20 years and in a relationship for 13 years, and I had full knowledge of her mental health the entire time. At least I thought I did; clearly, though, I knew only the tip of the iceberg. In the letter she said that she told me she was at work but then she would go out to binge. Sometimes she would frequent fast food restaurants and all-you-can-eat buffets while at other times she would just load up the car with food from the grocery store. She would sit in her car and eat enough food for 10 people, then purge.

I read all of this and felt horribly sad for her. I thought about the loneliness and desperation that she had been experiencing in those moments. After all we had been through to help her, none of it was getting better; in fact, it was getting worse. I asked her where she would go to do this, and she told me she couldn't remember because she would black out or just have a complete disconnection to her actions. Of all of the things she had to say, it was her last answer that bothered me most.

"You blacked out?" I asked. She nodded.

"You don't know where you were? Were you alone?"

She started to cry and replied, "I don't know."

My heart sank. It was so sad. All of the devotion and love and support; all of the years of protecting her and picking her up off the floor, and that's where we were at: "I don't know."

As the days passed I thought about the hundreds of phone calls telling me she'd be late, and I wondered how many "I don't knows" were involved. A few? A hundred? My mind constantly wondered about where she went, what she actually did, and whether she was alone. If she had lied to me so convincingly for such a long period of time, what was to stop her from telling more lies?

I actually tried to make peace and forgive her. I thought I could, but I couldn't. After this admission, I couldn't trust her with anything. Each day I became less trusting and less forgiving. If she told me the sky was blue, I would go check for myself. The feelings of resentment also grew. For so many years I had put her needs first. I supported her, encouraged her to greater happiness, and stood by her even though she was confronting serious health problems. I could have left a long time ago, but I didn't. I had stayed through so many dark days and nights and now, here I was, feeling like a sucker. I had been deceived on a daily basis. Every day, I would look at her and wonder where the next lie was. After a time, I knew that this was no way for either of us to live. Two decades of friendship had ended, and we went our separate ways.

Like many that go through a divorce, I was living in a state of disillusionment and melancholy. You're never really certain what to feel. You're constantly questioning whether it was the right decision.

I was in this exact state of disenchantment when I saw a car racing toward me as I crossed an intersection. I knew my light was green but I also knew that the car headed straight for me was not slowing down. It's quite an experience to watch two thousand pounds of steel hit you when the only thing separating you is a window and a door. I remember tensing and leaning into it, instinctively thinking I might stand a chance at stopping it with my shoulder. Well, it wasn't a linebacker and this wasn't pick-up football in the park. The car plowed me directly into a telephone poll.

I was lucky to be able to walk away from that accident.

I didn't break anything but I had plenty of pain. It would be difficult to walk over the next couple of months.

Shortly thereafter, as if being scripted for TV, right on cue, I received another incredulous surprise.

I discovered that the senior partner and principal founder of our turnaround consulting firm was keeping a second set of accounting books.

In our firm we had a practice of getting a deposit at the beginning of every engagement. Unlike law firms that typically bill weekly against a retainer and then replenish when empty, we held the deposit until the end of the engagement. When the last invoice was billed, we would generally deduct it against the deposit and return the remainder. In a consulting firm that specializes in working with distressed companies, things often slip through the cracks. In a crisis, things get lost or forgotten. The principal founder discovered that clients often forgot about their deposits. He would send them a final invoice, they'd pay it, and he wouldn't remind them about their security deposit. Unless they explicitly asked for it, he wouldn't return it, despite the fact that returning the deposit was clearly delineated in our contract.

When I discovered that one of my clients had not received his deposit nearly two months after the end of an engagement, I asked the senior partner about it, and he made no effort to hide his scam. He explained it to me in great detail and was proud of this balance sheet enhancement. He gleefully told me he'd been doing this for years. When I asked how much he had put aside, he informed me that it was a few hundred thousand dollars, and he showed me the list. Most of the clients were from before I joined the firm but there were a handful that were recent. I was upset but I looked for a solution to this problem.

I looked at him and said, "You screwed up. But that's okay. What you did in the past is the past. But now, we cannot do this again. We're going to return all of it, right now."

However, in complete disgust, he said, "There's no way we are returning it."

He then explained that some of the companies were no longer in existence and wondered who we would send the money to. I suggested that we find creditors that had not received full repayment of their loans and offer them the money. If not them, then the employees who got short-changed when the company was closed. If not them, then any suppliers that had lost. In my mind, there was a long list of people that were entitled to this money. Essentially, everyone but us should have the money.

However, he dug in his heels and said, "We earned that money."

I asked, "If we earned it, why have you been hiding this information? Why didn't you just invoice for the services delivered?" I received no response.

Since I was getting nowhere with him, I went to the other partners in the firm, but their consensus was to let sleeping dogs be. I explained to them that I would call and tell people that we discovered an accounting error and this money needed to be returned. The more options I offered, the more resistance I received. The senior partner was defiant, and the others were lazy and cowardly. They had to think about their reputations and how to explain all of this once it was made public. They knew that the odds of anyone else finding this money was slim, so why make a fuss about it? In my mind, this was theft, but they believed it was something else. I'm not sure what they thought it was, but it was accounting. It was black and white. It was a number that went into a box that didn't belong to us.

It was now very clear to me that I could no longer be a part of this firm. I couldn't understand any of the behavior. We were very profitable, very successful, and trusted at high levels, so why take this money from struggling and suffering people? Why not return it? What would they do with the money? Distribute it amongst the partners? Why the greed? They had enough. How much is enough? None of this made sense and none of it was in my moral compass. I knew that small problems would become big problems. If they could take this money, what would they take next? If they could sleep easily with this act, it would only give them more resolve for the next one, and I wanted no part of it. I had learned my lesson from the past. If I went along with this, I was equally to blame for any consequences.

After my years of hard work and great success in helping to build the firm, I decided to walk away. I resigned and gave up my partnership stake. I hated having to leave many of my colleagues. They were very talented and of high ethics. I was upset at the notion of having to start over again, but like Russia, it was a path I wasn't willing to follow. In Russia, there had been a clear line of criminality. Here, in the USA, it was a bit more ambiguous for some. But for me, to operate in this manner was a cold, soulless, and cowardly journey.

For most people, by this point, it would have seemed like it was enough—enough suffering, enough surprises, and enough loss. It was too much. In less than seven months, I lost my wife and my firm and had been plowed into a telephone pole by a speeding car. God, the Universe, Fate, Science, Human Nature…whomever was responsible, I thought they proved their point and would now move on.

But that wasn't the case. It was only August—five more months left in this very long year.

My next car accident bordered on comical. It was as if God was taking a popcorn break from dramatic cinema.

The chiropractor looked at me and said, "You're in good shape again." He was conducting the final physical examination after my treatments for the first car accident. He said I was good to go. I felt good to go. I walked out the door a healthy man. Five minutes later I was T-boned again, just outside his office. Only this time it was on the passenger side of the car. This one, I didn't see coming. I bounced around like a beat-up rag doll.

The police came, they filed a report, my car was towed away, and then I walked back into the chiropractor's office for a brand-new examination and treatment.

The lawyers for the two accidents wrung their hands with joy; they knew that no doctor or judge could determine exactly which car accident had caused which injury. As such, despite the extensive ligament and soft tissue damage in my back and hips, I had to settle each case for basic expenses.

When I wasn't with my chiropractor, I was with my internist and naturopath. My immune system had come close to a complete collapse through another strange set of circumstances. A bad rotisserie chicken left me fighting several different parasites, and a bad root canal left me filled with mercury. To heal myself I had to begin rounds of antibiotics and a three-month process of detoxing by administering chelation IVs, in which I was administered an amino acid intravenously that would bind with the toxins to help remove them. Three times a week I sat among cancer patients and people who had been exposed to large amounts of toxins, such as firemen. It was a grueling process, and I learned that toxins can be more harmful when they are leaving your body then when they entered. If you're not careful, the process can cause more damage—and even death.

So, I continued on in this manner, always seeming to visit the dark side of life. Now it had crossed over from my business dealings into my personal life; not just with my interactions with others but in my relationship with my own body. I was in constant physical pain that involved my back, my nervous system, and my immune system. But Life wasn't finished with me yet. The final stick in the eye would turn out to be an *actual* stick in the eye.

In late fall of 2002, I developed acute keratoconus, an eye disease that causes the cornea to weaken and morph. One day I had 20/20 vision and then the next I had 20/1600, with no prospect of ameliorating it with contact lenses or glasses. For some, a contact lens can be customized to fit but, in my case, it couldn't. After consulting with three separate ophthalmologists, they all concluded that I would go blind and eventually require a cornea transplant for each eye. For all intents and purposes, I could not see out of my left eye. They told me that my right eye could go at any time too, but they weren't certain when that might happen. It could be in 10 minutes or 10 years.

I was 35 years old. I had no wife, no company, and lousy health, and now I was well on my way to being legally blind. Welcome to adversity.

I lay on the floor in my living room and cursed out God, Jesus, the Universe, and everyone else I could think of. I was furious. All the studying in the world could not give me answers to what had just happened over the course of the year. It was as if some greater power had decided to endlessly torture me. I started to believe that I was cursed. That my life was just one giant cycle of pain and misery.

I yelled at the air, "I give up. Kill me. Just do it. You win. Take me out. Just KILL ME!"

I felt as if I had nothing to lose, not even faith. I had lost any sense of optimism or hope. The only certainty I had was that some degree of pain was headed my way. It hurt to walk, to eat, and now, even to see.

I wasn't prepared to kill myself. I figured if there was a grand design to this torture, I'd eventually die. I spent months wallowing in self-pity, anger, and fear, resenting everyone and everything. I made lists of everything I had lost and would lose. I couldn't figuratively and literally see a future for myself. I didn't know what I would do. My mind continually raced with thoughts that I would be physically and financially dependent on other people for the rest of my life. I couldn't understand how I went from leading people to having to be carried by them. I was convinced that there was no good answer except that I was meant to die young. So, day after day, I beat myself up with regrets as I waited for more bad news. I was certain that my death was imminent.

While waiting for my own funeral, I continued to ask questions. How did I miss so much? How did I miss my wife lying to me every single day for a year? How did I miss the senior partner keeping a separate set of financial records? Why all of the greed? How did people close to me cheat and betray me again? Why all of the car accidents? Why my vision? I counted on my eyes for everything. I needed them to study people, to make eye contact, and to read the room. I needed them to make friends and to understand how to connect with people. Gone were the days of business development conferences, intense meetings, and even driving a car. Gone were the days of taking referral sources out golfing—I couldn't see the ball. Worse still, I had developed intense vertigo, so I had to stop most outdoor activities. Even walking was a challenge. I had to wear an eye patch over my left eye to avoid bumping into things or falling down as I walked.

Eventually, reluctantly, I accepted that I wasn't dead. After months of beating myself up, I decided it was enough. I was getting nowhere complaining to myself and an invisible deity. I had to do something, anything.

I threw my laptop in the garbage and I put all of my books in storage. I decided that I was done with the business world. None of it mattered to me anymore. I didn't have any answers for my life experiences and none seemed to be coming soon. I just thought, *"I have to get out of here. There has to be a better way to live."*

I was looking for a dramatic change so I decided to go as far away from my current life as I could find on a map.

So, a couple of weeks after I made that decision, on New Year's Eve of 2002, I boarded a plane.

Four days later I was in a mud hut in Outer Mongolia, 50 miles from the Kazakhstan border and 90 miles from the Siberian border. I had taken up residence with a family of nomads. I was fascinated by the way they lived, and I wanted to understand how they still chose to exist with little technology and few possessions. The entire world was chasing more and better, but these people were content to live as they had for thousands of years. I wanted to know why they were living a life that seemed to be the polar opposite of mine.

By day, on horseback, we would hunt with eagles. Similar to falconry, we would release an eagle that preyed on fox or rabbit. It was an activity the Mongols had been engaged in for more than 2,000 years. It was meant to help the long, cold winters pass a bit easier. We would ride four to six hours a day in temperatures that hovered around 20 below. At night, it would drop to 35 below freezing. Despite wearing multiple layers of high-tech clothing and wrapping up in a sophisticated sleeping bag, I was still cold. We had a stove that was lit early evening that warmed the hut until roughly 2 a.m., but once that fire went out, it was bitter cold until it was re-lit around 8 a.m. I tried hand warmers, several hats, three pairs of socks, but I couldn't stay comfortable. Finally, after a few days of watching my hosts I realized that maybe I should do what they do. They looked cozy all day and all night. Wool was the solution. They gave me one of their hats, a coat, and several wool carpets. The hat and coat kept me warm with only one layer while on horseback. And, at night, I covered myself in carpets, I was as comfortable as I could ever be. It was a great lesson in paying attention to your surroundings and adapting accordingly. No technology could create products better than nature.

During the day, we ate very little—only a piece of rye bread, a sardine, and some tea. At night, we had boiled horse meat. The Mongols and their children liked music, so each night I would put portable, air-activated hand warmers on small speakers and my CD player and play an album. They liked Sinatra and Enya the best.

The Mongols were extremely peaceful. They spoke in whispers—they had no need to raise their voices. The next nearest home was five hours away. There were no roads, no cars, no electricity, and no phones. There was no semblance of the typical Western world. It was quiet all day and all night.

They taught me a great deal about living in harmony

with nature and with each other. They looked each other in the eye when they spoke. They listened with complete attention, and they were extremely mindful of each other's well-being. Every day they would sing to their horses, goats, and each other. When it got too cold outside, they brought the goats into their home to protect them from the frigid temperature. Their eagle was fed indoors like a family pet. They were without politics or religion and they didn't believe in fences. They had very few possessions, but they were as happy as you could ever imagine. When I asked them if they were ever curious about traveling to the world outside of theirs, they politely said "no" and explained that they had everything they wanted right there. They had a sense of contentment and longed for nothing. I admired them and aspired to be more like them. I had spent years chasing and climbing. I had spent an equal amount of time losing and falling. Perhaps I needed to try it their way; content and at peace with whatever was around me.

When I returned home, that calm presence from the Mongols stayed with me. Every day, I became more captivated with the path toward peace and silence. I spent months learning about monks who devote their lives to prayer, work, and silence. I read books about Thomas Merton, a well-known monk who wrote extensively about incorporating many different practices of faith. He had worked hard to show the similarities in different religions. His focus was on bringing people together in a common pursuit: peace.

Thomas Merton spent many years at a Benedictine monastery, the Abbey of Gethsemane, which was situated on 2,500 acres in Trappist, Kentucky. I made several visits to the Abbey over a period of a few years. I was intrigued as to why anyone would choose to live in seclusion with minimal dialogue and go to mass nine times a day. I wanted to know what it would feel like to sing the Psalms all day, every day, and then spend the rest of the time alternating between doing physical work and being alone in quiet reflection. No phones or computers were allowed. Once you checked in as a visitor, your name was erased from the reservation book the objective was to be private and nondescript. Any clothing with images or messaging was also prohibited.

Over time, as I walked the property, read, and went to mass, I learned to live in prayer and silence. The quiet was unsettling at first, but then I came to seek it out. The more silence I experienced the more I wanted to experience it. I then started to visit the monastery for longer retreats. On one visit, the monks invited me to use their personal retreat space, a hermitage. Deeper into their property stood a simple home. Monks would leave the monastery for this cabin when they felt they needed to go further into their prayer and silence.

Like the Mongols, the Benedictines were extremely peaceful and nonjudgmental. Over the entrance to the monastery, written in cement, were the words "God Alone." They believe that no one can tell you how to get through this world; that it is between you and God alone. For me, this was a profound message. In my life, up until then, someone was always telling me how to live. It was either a religion or it was Madison Avenue or family, friends, colleagues, partners. Everyone had the answer to what I needed to do in order to be happy, fulfilled, and redeemed in the afterlife. But now, I had met a group of men who had been living in continuous prayer since the fourth century and had a different belief. They said to me and everyone else that came to their door,

"We're here to give you a place to rest and eat. How you live is between you and God."

In prayer, I spent most of my time forgiving others and praying for their well-being. But outside of prayer there was this message: "It's just you and God." It was an interesting dichotomy. Like most learning, one answer leads to more questions. At least, that's how it was for me. I came to learn that God is about two things: love and life—mostly the love of life. We have the freedom to choose how we want to live, but what is most important is that we live and respect the life in others.

I continued on like this for a few years, delving deeper into spiritual and environmental worlds and studying life and practices that had carried over thousands of years—sometimes billions of years. I was trying to experience a greater resonance with life; trying to understand how to heal myself and heal others. I spent a lot of time in nature studying the natural, uninterrupted flow of life. As business leaders we are constantly trying to make order. We put things into a lot of boxes and rows and categories. We're always straightening, analyzing, and reshaping and creating direction through strategy and mission. At this point in my life, I wanted to do none of that. I just wanted to observe and let be.

The more I looked at nature, the more clearly I understood the importance of inter-connectedness. Everything in the sky, land, and ocean had a purpose. Everything touched each other and helped the other grow. Often, one thing—one entity—had many functions and served many roles. There were days I would just look at a tree and wonder at how many things it does. It provides shade, shelter for birds and squirrels and their nests, a highway for ants and other bugs, branches for firewood, and oxygen for us to breathe. It even serves as a urinal for dogs. It sounded basic and simple, but it was anything but. It was teaching me to pay attention, to look closer with an open mind and see the value of life in all things living.

After years of studying peace and harmony, I went in the other direction; I wanted to learn more about pain. I then began a long journey reading and talking with those who help heal others: EMT, doctors, therapists, and trauma specialists. I spent a lot of time with a trauma specialist who eventually became a good friend. He has treated more than 16,000 people who have been through every possible trauma imaginable—physical, emotional, mental, and spiritual. He had treated people from the Oklahoma bombing and 9/11. He helped me understand the neurology behind the physical trapping of pain and how it manifests in erratic and debilitating behavior.

I learned that most of our traumas are hidden from us and that they only present themselves when we are ready to deal with them. They first manifest in annoyances and then escalate to throbbing, unshakeable pain. Eventually, if not dealt with, they result in deterioration of the cells in the body. Within time, it will manifest some form of disease. I learned the importance of shining light on problems and going to the source of their origin. It was a journey not to be feared. It was one to be celebrated. Once free of the trauma, our mind, body, and being is clear to experience new things in life. He had an incredible gift for helping guide people to release these traumas.

Despite working with me for years, we could never conclude exactly why I had lost my vision in such a dramatic fashion. Maybe my soul had seen too much suffering, or maybe my eyes had too much exposure to the sun. I didn't know. The only thing that was clear was that my vision continued to worsen in both eyes.

As my vision weakened, my other senses became more sensitive and alert. My sense of hearing, smell, taste, and touch increased dramatically. I learned to turn off my head and live in my body and often would spend entire days with my eyes closed. I would just feel my way through my surroundings.

I became so sensitive that I threw out all of my soaps, cleaning supplies, colognes, pillows, blankets, and clothing. I needed soft, warm, neutral-smelling, nontoxic items around me; otherwise, I would be overwhelmed. As I interacted with other people, I found myself becoming exhausted easily. In the past I could spend countless hours around large groups of people and be reinvigorated. Now, I would be wiped out in an hour. Every sound, scent, and motion would enter my body. It was as if I had become a tuning fork. I became so sensitive to the outside world that I could feel the intensity of emotion from people who were a couple of feet away from me. It was tiring but fascinating. My physical change was making me become a different person at multiple levels. I moved slower. I no longer raced by. If I wanted to see a person's face, I had to get closer and actually stare at it. The closer I got, the more I saw and the more I felt. At first this was uncomfortable, but as time passed it became normal. It made me empathize with people at a deeper level.

As time passed, the amalgam of studying nature, religion, and humanity, combined with all of the changes within my physical body, completely converged. The resentment and anger had left me. I was at a new level of comfort with the world. There were days that I gave serious consideration to following the path of Thomas Merton, becoming a monk, living a life of prayer and sharing with others. It was tranquil and non-confrontational. Why not try that path in life?

Then, one day, out of the blue, my life changed again. My vertigo subsided, and the world stopped spinning. I was still legally blind, but I could function. I could walk without falling down. I could actually look at a computer screen without getting completely dizzy. It was better, but my range of vision was still severely limited. Essentially, it was completely blurred except for a circle the size of a small Frisbee directly in front of me. If I moved my head from side to side too quickly, I couldn't see a thing, but I could function. I would still have to pack my face in ice at night, though. The eye strain would make the facial muscles inflame, but I could live with this level of discomfort. Now, all of a sudden, I had a resurgence in my outlook for life. I could be a monk, but I also could do other things. I had taken a three-year hiatus from the working world, but now I felt it was the right time to return.

With my newfound consciousness and my new body, I was reluctant to return to crisis management. I just thought, "It was a good experience but I'm not going back to that craziness. It's too hard. There has to be more comfortable ways of earning a living." I began looking for work in teaching and government. I was looking for anything non-confrontational. I spent a couple of months exploring options and applying for positions, but nothing clicked. I had a lot of interest, but I didn't get any offers. Then one day, a former competitor called and said he heard that I was back on the market. He wanted to know if I was interested in a job with his firm. The new, peaceful part of me thought, "Let's just see what he has to say." I kept an open mind and met with him.

His firm was different from my previous firm. There were no young and dynamic employees. They were established consultants and a group of decent, good people who came from a wide array of industries in the corporate world. They were older and had a lot of experience. I was now 39. If I took a position with them, I would be the youngest in the firm. I thought maybe I could benefit from their years of accumulated wisdom.

I went away and thought about the offer and opportunity. As much as I wanted nothing to do with crisis management and warring with people, I still had unfinished business within myself. I wanted one more chance to use all of my skills to run a company, but this time I wanted to work on more complex problems and run bigger companies. I also wanted to test all my newfound spiritual skills in the business world. I wanted to spread peace and gratitude in otherwise difficult environments. I was older and wiser and I thought I could use my new level of maturity, patience, and understanding to help others. I had found purpose in my adversity. I overcame it and I thought, *Okay, it's time. I'm ready for the next challenge. Let's see what life has for me now.* I accepted the job and took my old suits and dress shoes out for a thorough dusting.

It was now the fall of 2006. The economy was doing great. People were feeling rich and invincible. Everyone seemed generous and optimistic. I felt like a babe in the woods. I had been absent from the business world for more than three years. I took meetings, shook hands, and had many nights of happy, networking dinners. It seemed like good times were here to stay. But, my inner voice and newfound peace had no idea of the massive economic collapse that was headed our way.

Within a couple months, there were signs that a dramatic

shift in the financial markets had started. The projects that came to us were exhibiting bold symptoms of rapid and massive decline. They had skipped past underperforming and had gone directly to walking corpse.

I had a new client that was the perfect harbinger to the national economic collapse that would crush many in the coming years.

I walked through the 150,000-square-foot building and I saw and heard no one. I was confused; it was the middle of the week in the middle of the day. I had confirmed my meeting a few days earlier. There were supposed to be 200 employees at this one division.

I called out, "Hello? Hello?"

I kept walking and walking, and I *called out* again, "Hello? Hello?"

An older gentleman appeared in the distance and began to walk toward me. We introduced ourselves—his name was Tim. I asked Tim where everybody was, and he said they weren't there because they had no work to do.

I was very confused. This company was supposed to be building machines. It was supposed to be generating approximately $55M in annual revenue, averaging close to a million a week. How could there be no work?

We walked to Tim's office. He looked beaten and worn out and he didn't offer any explanations or additional conversation. Finally, I asked him what his salesmen were doing. He told me he had only one salesman, and that he was making phone calls at the moment. I then asked what prospects he had in his pipeline, and he told me they had two prospects that they were hoping to close. I was shocked. They were supposed to be making a few machines a week and now there was virtually nothing. They would have made more money mowing lawns or hosting a bake sale.

I left my meeting with Tim and went to call his lender. They were owed more than $16M, but the bank had no idea the company was in this bad of a condition. No one from the bank had been on site for more than two years.

Tim was in his early 60s with a business degree and an MBA from Ivy League schools. He'd had a storied career in management and he'd capped it by overseeing a successful roll-up of multiple companies in the machine building industry. He had sold his company and retired in his 50s. Life was good.

After a few years of playing endless rounds of golf and telling the same stories to the same friends, Tim decided that he'd end his boredom. He thought he'd try one more roll-up. He'd use his time-tested style and knowledge to make more money, buy a bigger home and custom-made golf clubs, and have new stories for the old friends.

He set his eyes upon three separate machine companies that had been in business between 20 and 100 years. He'd buy all of them, merge operations, and maximize synergies. He approached the owners, put together financing, cut a fair deal, and was off to a great start. He projected increasing revenue by 40% within three years. He would flip the company in the fourth year and he would be back on the links in no time.

Unfortunately, Tim's timing couldn't have been worse. He literally got hit with a perfect managerial storm. Twelve months after he closed the deal, demand in his industry slowed, and technological changes allowed for customers to buy his products off-shore for a fraction of the cost. Then the union contract expired, and the entire workforce went on strike.

He spent nine months of his second year of ownership negotiating his way out of the strike with the union. By the time they came to a new agreement, the entire world around him had changed. Demand for his products was whimpering along, and his customers had changed their buying habits. Nonetheless, Tim was stuck with all of this debt. In addition to what he owed his senior lender, he owed $26M to the previous owners. With the trade and accrued interest, he owed close to $50M, and he had ONE salesman and virtually no sales prospects.

After a couple of weeks of searching, slicing and dicing, analyzing, and exploring options to restart this company, there was nothing that looked feasible. However, there was one bright light that remained in the distance. Their replacement parts division that was located in another state still had revenue and generated profits. It had been treated as an abandoned orphan for years because it didn't have the dynamic growth potential of the other divisions. However, it was a classic tortoise and the hare story. It was small and moved slowly but it was profitable.

The principal machines manufactured by this company had not significantly changed in design in 50 years. Between the three companies, there were thousands of their machines in companies all around the world. Those machines would eventually need parts for repair. There were thousands of possible parts and people would need to buy them from somewhere. There was no good reason to close this division when it had a large and existing customer base.

We came up with a plan to liquidate all of the nonperforming assets and then reorganize as a machine repair and replacement part company. Our projections forecast that the senior lender would eventually be paid out over the course of the next five years. For us, this was a great win. We found something positive out of the ashes. It would be a much smaller company but it would still generate millions in revenue and slowly but steadily pay off the bank's debt.

Furthermore, theoretically, after the senior lender was paid, the other debtholders and owners could continue to operate and/or sell the company. The previous owners might never get paid in full but at least there was a chance at some recovery. There's always a chance with a profitable company. It seemed like a good strategy.

The day before we were scheduled to meet the bank in New York City, my contact at the bank called and asked me to send a copy of our assessment and plan to him in advance. I didn't have a problem with this. Bankers hate surprises. Many of them like to review the details before the actual meeting.

The next morning, we arrived at the bank, eager to meet with the credit team to review the plan. Instead what we found was that there would be no "team." There was just a guy—my guy. He walked into the conference room and asked me to come into his office. I followed him 20 feet down the hall into his corner office. He sat behind his desk and said, "Ummm, yeah, so...we've decided to liquidate the entire company."

I was stunned. "What? Why? Did you read the plan? It's a good plan. You get 100% recovery in five years with virtually no added risk. If you liquidate, you'll probably lose $10 million or more." He put his head down and said, "I know. It's a reasonable plan. You guys did a good job. But, this entire thing has to go away—fast." I was so confused. "Why?" He started to sweat and became very nervous "Listen, I will tell you but I will deny it if word ever gets out. I just don't want to lose my job."

He then went on to explain to me that the banker originally assigned to this loan—the same guy who didn't visit, didn't audit, and wasn't around to see its decline—was a rising "star" in the bank. He was the heir to the throne. They were grooming him for a top leadership position so they needed to hide all of his mistakes. And, this was a big mistake.

If the banker had done his job and actually visited the company, the loan would have been reduced gradually over time. The company would have been forced to make reductions sooner. In other words, the problems could have been managed when they were smaller. Certainly, Tim could have done this himself. He was equally culpable for the company's demise. But, now, all of that was behind us. We had an actual plan that could pay off the bank loan in its entirety and save some jobs for years to come. But that would never happen. They would put the final nail in the coffin of this company, and write off approximately $10M to protect this one banker's "good name." What a farce.

So, just like that, a viable reorganization, jobs, and millions of dollars were erased. By liquidating quickly, the company and its loan would be removed from the bank's "current accounts" list. The names would disappear. The actual dollar amount of the loss would be put in the big pile of "write-off" of losses for the bank. No one would ever question it again. And, then, the absentee banker who had helped ruin the company and lose millions could seem smarter and better than he actually was for the rest of his career.

I finished that project knowing that something was really

wrong in the business and banking world. I had been gone for three years but it felt like an eternity. Business was supposed to be practical and measured, but now I was starting to see extremes. I knew this type of thinking and behavior was very destructive. Unfortunately, there was a lot more of it to come.

In the summer of 2007, I was appointed chief restructuring officer of a $150M Tier One automotive supplier. This was my first CRO position. I had just turned 40. By now, I had significant experience in business but for me this was an entirely new level of managerial challenges.

There were three principal locations and approximately 1,400 employees. The company had fallen out of favor with its primary customer, one of the Big Three auto manufacturers. However, this supplier was critical because it supplied 52% of all of this OEM's plants in North America. The OEM could not afford to have this company fail or falter in the least bit. For me, it was an honor to be in this position. It was clearly the biggest company that I had ever been asked to manage. However, it was also the most politically charged and complicated I had ever been involved with because of so many different competing interests. The company was owned by a private equity division of a major bank. Banks can't lend to companies they own, so two other banks were involved in the deal. Being a fairly large supplier, there were also other OEMs involved as customers. Essentially, I was sandwiched in between a herd of elephants—a lot of big players and all their lawyers and financial advisors.

Making it more complicated was the constant battle for cash and materials to build the auto parts. The golden rule in the automotive industry is to never shut down a primary production line. If you do, it can cost anywhere from $20,000 to $50,000 per minute. In this environment, you can lose a million dollars quickly. So, no questions asked, you have to have your parts at the OEM's plants on time, every day. The ticking of the clock never escapes you. Whatever you have to do to be on time, you do. This particular company was under so much financial pressure that they had resorted to war-like survival tactics. But they had to; this was Detroit.

Detroit historically operates primarily with power and intimidation. Decades of fighting amongst each other and with unions created a tough town. This situation was no different. The typical OEM works like this: *Do what we tell you or you're out.* For example, in this case, they forced my client to produce at least 10% of their parts for new cars at a loss. Parts they produced as replacements for old-model cars were forced to be made at an even greater loss. When the company asked for an increase in price or asked to stop making those parts, the response was simple: "If you don't make those parts at the price we want, you won't get any new work at the better margins." So, you had little to no choice; you took the work or you worked in another industry.

However, even when you took the work, if the OEM decided they didn't like you for whatever reason, they started to pay their invoices slowly. Then they started to find fault with your products. The goal was to pay you slowly and shave your invoice down. Over time, margins collapse, cash becomes tighter and tighter, and the company moves into survival mode. Everyone throughout your company finds ways to get by. Mid-level production managers know that there isn't enough money to buy supplies, so they ask for significantly more materials, hoping to get "something" when their request is whittled down. People in finance start to burn out. Complaints mount from every direction. Suppliers start changing their payment terms from 60 to 30 to COD and, ultimately, CIA—cash in advance. Eventually, you just don't have enough money to buy supplies to make parts.

This is precisely what happened in this situation. It's what happens when your customer has too much power over your business. Unwilling to give my client price increases on parts, the OEM forced them into a Chapter 11 bankruptcy filing. They decided that they wanted the company sold through the bankruptcy courts. They intended to steer the sale toward someone they preferred to work with. It had nothing to do with quality of work. It was all about personalities not getting along. My client refused to bend any further so they fought back and the OEM didn't take kindly to a minion not towing the line. In the end, this high-level spat would cost them tens of millions of dollars and cost my client at least a hundred million in lost value. A brutal example of unnecessary waste.

However, despite being a difficult situation, I was a new CRO and my intention was to put to use my managerial skills. I was young and I felt like perhaps I could inject some positive changes in this otherwise hostile environment. I wanted to implement many of the engineering best practices I had learned over the years. I thought it would be best to start implementing them right before we filed for bankruptcy. I thought that we would go into court and put our best foot forward for the judge, demonstrating a good-faith attempt to increase value for all of the unsecured creditors that might not otherwise get paid. So, we began by consolidating two facilities, which involved laying off some employees—fairly straightforward techniques that seemed harmless.

Two days later I would appear in bankruptcy court testifying to the circumstances that had led to the filing. Despite the tensions between the owner, customer, and banks, we were able to present a reasonable plan that satisfied senior secured creditors. All went as planned, and I left the courthouse feeling that we were off to a good start.

On my way back to the plant, I received a phone call from the CEO. He had just received a phone call from the state police. We were informed that one of the employees I had laid off had just killed his wife and stepson. He was missing and now the police believed he was coming for us next. This was my first big job—my first attempt at a managerial clean-up. It resulted in double homicide, and now I was being hunted. I should have been afraid, but I wasn't. I was annoyed. My bigger concern was for the other employees. If this employee was truly disgruntled, who knew what he was capable of next? He had already proven that he could kill two people. How many more would there be?

The police sent cruisers to the plant and to the homes of the CEO and CFO. I was living in a hotel during the week, which made it difficult to figure out where I was staying, so we thought I might be okay. There wasn't much else that we could do other than wait. We worked and prayed that he wouldn't hurt anyone else.

Five days later police found him 10 states over, on a bike with a duffle bag full of guns. He was disgruntled but he had greater mental health issues.

Those murders set the fearful and stressful tone for the duration of the project. The company was given so little cash in our budget that there was a lot of pressure to keep everything working on a just-in-time basis with no room to spare. We had people standing on the docks waiting for supplies, then running to machines to start production. At the other end, we had several pilots on stand-by in case we needed to fly parts to plants. We did anything to keep the OEM's primary assembly lines moving.

Our finance department had dwindled to only a couple of people—brave and intelligent women who were the only ones who had the right answers to questions. One of them confided in me that the stress was getting to them and they were thinking of quitting. They asked me if I was okay with them taking Xanax or Valium. I told them if it helped them, I had no issues.

Every day was a fight for parts. The amount of money that we actually had to spend would be calculated each morning. Generally, by 10 a.m. the bank would send over the borrowing base certificate that showed the amount of parts we shipped and the eligible account receivables we had generated. On average, we had $700k-$800k to buy parts. At the same time, every day, managers from all of the plants would send a list to the CFO of the materials they absolutely needed. Every morning this list showed a purchase list that totaled on average $2M-$2.5M. When I first saw this phenomenon, I panicked. I thought there was no way the company could survive. The CFO, having lived this way for almost two years, knew who was lying and by how much. Deftly, he would swipe through the list, changing all of the numbers. This practice went on for the entire duration of the case. Finance and production existed in this manner but everything else was at a virtual standstill.

I had the most senior title and the most responsibility, but every time I wanted to do something I needed the approval of more than a dozen people. If I wanted to sell scrap metal, I needed the bank's lawyers, the OEM's lawyers, our lawyers, and the unsecured creditors' lawyers—and all of their financial advisors—to sign off. If someone determined that 30 cents on the dollar was not enough for that scrap metal, then it couldn't be sold. It didn't matter that no one would actually pay more than that. It only mattered that people had the power to say "no."

Months passed living in this quagmire. We were spending countless hours debating the most insignificant pieces of data, and tens of millions of dollars were being wasted on administration of the obvious. Meanwhile, hundreds of legitimate suppliers were going to be completely stiffed on their outstanding debt. They had made and shipped parts in good faith and now they weren't going to be paid. There was one long chain of people being cheated just because someone at the top didn't like someone else. This wasn't business; this was something else. It felt like war in Cambodia. The people, the language, the fighting…all were strange. All were dangerous and unpredictable. As each month passed I wondered, *Why? What was the point to all of this?* My own deeper Zen and outreach to the spiritual world was slipping away. Then, one day, I think it just left. I woke up and felt nothing.

We were in the fifth month of this planned six-month bankruptcy. The principal OEM had financed a significant portion of the bankruptcy as the DIP (Debtor in Possession) lender. My client's company was not unionized; most of the employees were single moms earning between $12 and 14 per hour. There were three locations with more than 1,500 employees. At the end of the bankruptcy, it was unclear how many would have jobs. The intent was that the assets would be sold to another supplier, but it was unclear whether they would absorb all of the employees.

At the beginning of the bankruptcy, the OEM agreed to pay for all of the worker's compensation claims and health insurance claims. The company plans were self-funded. When an employee gets injured it takes weeks, sometimes months, for the claims to be processed. This meant that after the bankruptcy and sale of assets were completed, there would be trailing liabilities. These would have to be funded or else the healthcare providers (doctors, therapists, hospitals, etc.) would go after the employee for the money, even if the company no longer existed.

Five months had passed, and the OEM kept kicking this issue down the road. As CRO, I kept asking them to put this dollar amount in the budget to be approved by the bankruptcy judge, and each time they said they would do it later. This amount was approximately $1.5M. We were a month out from the closing of the sale and I now knew they had no intention of paying. They were tough and unrepentant. They would burn the employees and they figured the scorched earth would figure itself out. I wasn't okay with this. I figured we needed to resolve this matter quickly. Talking was getting nowhere; I had had enough of inaction. For months, despite holding the title of CRO, I felt like I had little control over anything. But there still were a few things that were within my reach. I needed to wake everyone up and get their attention.

At each plant, the OEM had half a dozen engineers monitoring all production. When a supplier is in trouble they no longer trust their representations, so they demand that their own people are present at these factories. They are the eyes and ears, ensuring that things are running smoothly. So, I decided to make the OEM blind and deaf. I called the plants and had my team escort these engineers to the door. I threw 18 of them to the curb at 3:30 p.m. That got their attention. It took 20 minutes for the OEM's lawyer in Detroit to call me.

"Did you throw all of my client's engineers out of your plant?" he asked.

"Yes."

"Why would you do that? It's illegal. We have an agreement. We will get an injunction."

I shot back, "That's a good idea. You should go to court. We should all go to court. I want to explain to the judge how you are cheating 1,500 employees out of their healthcare insurance and worker's compensation claims."

"We said that we'd pay those claims. We're going to pay them."

"Great. Pay them today."

"This is not the way to negotiate."

I replied, "It's not a negotiation," and hung up on him before he could respond.

Ten minutes later, my lawyer phoned me, and I hung up on him. Ten minutes after that, the bank's lawyer phoned me, and I hung up on him too. I then called my team at each plant. I told them to buy a disposable camera and go to the bar where these engineers were hanging out. Our plants were in small towns; I knew it would not be difficult to find them and I knew for certain they were drinking and probably laughing at my certain demise. I then instructed my team to take pictures of each one of them. Not in secret. I told them to walk up to them and snap a picture. Most posed and smiled.

Twenty minutes later, Detroit was on the phone again. This time there were three lawyers on the call. More muscle. The most senior lawyer began the conversation in a confused and almost hushed tone:

"Domenic, did you take pictures of all of my client's engineers?"

"Yes," I replied. "And I have pictures of you and your legal team too."

"Why? Why would you do that?" he questioned.

"I'm going to put all of the pictures on the company bulletin boards."

His voice tightened. "What exactly are you trying to do?"

"Well, in a couple of hours, all of the employees are going to find out that they're not going to have health insurance or worker's compensation. They're going to be really mad. They're going to want to kill people. I just want to make sure they kill the right people." I hung up the phone.

They phoned back 10 minutes later. They had a woman attorney start the conversation this time.

"Domenic, we already agreed to pay this amount so why are you doing this?"

"Jane," I replied. "I think you and your client are deceitful and have no intention of paying."

"Domenic, we can meet tomorrow and make the appropriate plans."

"Sorry, too late. I need the money today. If I don't have it today, I am shutting the plants down at midnight. If I don't have adequate insurance, I cannot in good conscience let people into the plants knowing that they might get hurt and there's no money to pay for their healthcare."

There was a long, silent pause. Then Jane responded.

"My client can't do that."

I hung up.

Jane called back immediately, yelling into the speaker phone.

"You are holding a gun to my client's head. This is no way to negotiate."

I burst out laughing. "Hey, I didn't ask to be Jimmy Hoffa. I'm not trying to form a union here. You made a deal—just honor the deal. Your client got parts for their cars. Pay your bills. These people worked in earnest for you and now you want to cheat them. This isn't a gun. A gun is a single mom showing up at an emergency room with her kid on a Saturday night thinking she has insurance. Then two months later when she's unemployed, she gets a bill for $1,500—THAT is a gun. Pay your bills or you don't get your parts."

I hung up.

Thirty minutes later $1.5M was wired into our account.

I didn't feel great about this. I didn't smile and high-five anyone. I just shook my head and thought, "How stupid." I knew how to street fight. I knew how to survive. I also knew how to protect people. I just thought that in a company this big and this important, that people would be straightforward and honorable, but they weren't.

The company did close a sale to a competitor a month later. The new owner kept approximately 1,000 employees. The OEM also agreed to price increases for the new owner. It was all negotiated in the backrooms before an offer for the purchase was officially presented. The OEM had been working with them for months planning this change of ownership. It was just about power. They could have given my client the same price increases but they didn't like their "tone" and "attitude" so they crushed them, just because they could. I was happy for the employees and the small towns where the factories were located; they managed to survive during a difficult economic climate. But, this job left me with an unsettled feeling.

Something in me changed. I had tried to be a diplomat for many years. I tried to be respectful and patient, but I kept getting burned. I kept losing companies to thieves and morally flexible scum. I was trying to help people. I was trying to save jobs and companies. I was tired of people dying, people losing jobs and homes, communities being ruined. So, I knew that I had to take a different approach. I knew that by threatening a line shutdown to a major automotive manufacturer I was effectively burning a bridge. They were tough and mean to innocent bystanders, and they were worse if you provoked them. I knew that they would now actively try to prevent me from ever getting work again in the automotive industry. My actions with the healthcare insurance cost me and my firm a great deal, but it didn't matter; I determined that from here forward, I would take a more aggressive position when it came to saving companies. Whatever peace and harmony I had found with the monks and Mongols had been put aside. I had no time for prayer beads. I made up my mind to fight harder and faster, and I did. But, the moment I made this decision to put on a new suit of armor, it was as if I was tempting the gods of finance for a battle. In the blink of an eye, the world became darker, uglier, and far more complicated.

By early summer of 2008, my phone was ringing so much that I didn't have time to answer it. I couldn't hire employees fast enough at our firm. Companies were falling out of the sky, and a world of panic, irrationality, greed, and abuse enveloped me and every client that I took on. In the next four years, I would be either CEO, CRO, or COO at three additional companies. Each company had sales greater than $125M and more than 1,000 employees. In total, from 2008 to 2012, I directly oversaw more than $700M in revenue, and managed more than 6,000 employees. In addition, I would advise on an another 45 clients, tens of thousands of employees, billions of revenue and debt.

Eighteen-hour days were the norm; it was the most

intense and hardest that I had ever worked, and I did all of it while legally blind. I was in a fog of war and all I could see with my limited vision was an actual fog.

I could not see someone's face if they were more than three feet away from me. Everything was a blur. I learned to walk and move methodically. Gone were the high-energy days of my younger years. I couldn't move fast because I would experience vertigo. Routinely, my head would spin and I would bump into chairs, desks, doors. If I turned my head too quickly, the blur would feel as if someone had spun me in a circle.

At times, it was very difficult to live with the physical impediment because it was a problem that I knew wouldn't go away. It was painful and debilitating but I tried to be positive so I made adjustments to adapt to my circumstances. I learned to put most of my energy into listening carefully and feeling the energy in people. I also concentrated my thoughts more intently. I became much better at memorizing numbers and events. I needed to remember facts and figures because I couldn't rely on my eyes to see them again.

When my eyes and vertigo were very bad, I would stay at home and take all my calls from my sofa, on my back. I would lie down, close my eyes, and just listen to the tone and nuances in everyone's voices. Their cadence and tone were as revealing as looking at the expressions on their face.

This was a time when everyone was losing something. Business owners were losing, but so were accountants, bankers, lawyers, and millions of employees. Jobs, savings accounts, and homes were being lost. People were angry, scared, and frustrated. They looked for people to blame and they grabbed at everything they could to save themselves. I was in the middle of all of this financial and emotional firestorm. It was my job to help them find reason and find a way out of this mountain of debt and loss. It was insane and unrelenting, but I was going to try as hard as I could to help as many as possible.

Lessons for Adversity

1. Thank Goliath.

The moment adversity is beset upon you, thank it. That challenge or obstacle, in whatever form it may be, is bringing you an opportunity to further help you to define yourself. No one would ever have remembered David's name if he had not fought Goliath. That mountain helped create an immortal legend out of David and a powerful story for all of us.

Task: What has challenged your business in the past? How did you overcome that adversity? Do you still resent what happened? Look at the issue or person and find the reason it made you better. When you do, say, "Thank you."

Whatever you are facing today, start each day and end each day by saying, "Thank you…you will only make me better." In that state of mind, you will find an answer and you won't destroy your body, soul, and mind—or others—in the process.

Lessons for Adversity

2. Uncertainty is waiting for you to discover it.

The answer is always there. Embrace the uncertainty. Somewhere in the confusion, in the darkness, there will be a window. Oftentimes, as children, we may have been afraid of the dark...that is, until the lights were turned on and we realized everything that made us feel safe was already there. The light is there; you just need to find the switch.

Task: What are you facing? What are you fearing? Look into that fear. Pick up a pen and write down the absolute truth of what can happen if your fears come true. Then, next to each point, write down what you can do to either prevent or mitigate damages. Then, each day, do something to implement those plans. Tell others, get help, talk less, do more, and uncertainty will become your friend.

Lessons for Adversity

3. You're not that smart. Get an independent assessment.

If you're facing trouble for an extended period of time, it's probably a result of your leadership decisions. If you helped create the problem, your thinking may not be the best to get you out of the problem. Seek out help. Seek out a true, independent assessment. Seek out specialists, creative thinkers, and advisors from different fields. Find people who think differently than you. Seeking help doesn't mean you're weak and you've failed. It means you're smart and proactive. There is tremendous power in a group focused on overcoming a problem.

Task: Go outside your circle of trusted friends. Do research on specialists and/or advisors from a different field. You've tried solving the problem your way, with your people; now try it another way. If it doesn't work the first time, try again. Keep trying a different approach from a different thinker until you get the right result.

Lessons for Adversity

4. Remember to get paid.

Many companies put extra pressure on themselves and get into trouble because they extend too much credit to their customers. Unless you are bank, don't act like one. Collect on your invoices immediately. Money shows respect. When people pay us for our products or services it tells that they value and respect what we did for them. Get paid or get rid of them as customers. Only work with those who appreciate you.

Despite the harsh environment I work in, I live by this credo. All of my clients are out of cash and their credit is maxed out the very first day I start working with them. Do you think I extend credit terms to them? Nope. I have a clear policy; my invoice for the previous week is delivered on Wednesday, I am paid by Friday...or, I don't show up on Monday. I really don't. I don't care how far underwater you are, if you are serious about saving your business and you respect me and my work—pay me.

And, everyone who works for me lives by this same policy. I add one extra condition for them so they help ensure that we get paid in a timely manner. It's quite simple: If I don't get paid, you don't get paid. This way, it's a team effort. In 20 years of working in distressed financial environments, there is only ONE invoice that I was unable to collect.

Task: Go through your account receivables. Line by line. Start making phone calls. You may hear every excuse in the world why they can't pay. They may cry, they may yell at you, they may threaten to never work with you again, they may rationalize why they shouldn't pay you in full—who cares? Be firm, be clear, and don't be afraid. You provided a service or a product, they benefited from it—you deserve to get paid.

Some will want discounts—don't do it. Discounts cheapen your company. Offer a discount only if you are desperate. Only if you absolutely need that cash today. A better option is just to take partial payments. If you're stuck and they're stuck too, have them give you "something" each week as an act of good faith. Do not let those receivables sit there without any regular pay down. They will eventually become dust, as will you.

Lessons for Adversity

5. The answers are on the front lines: Explore storefronts and shop-floors.

Sitting behind your desk reviewing financial statements or having endless meetings with senior executives in board rooms will only give you some of the facts. To make solid and complete decisions, you need to gather facts at the front lines. Wherever a product is "made," whether on the screen of a software engineer or the shop floor of a factory, listen closely to the "bakers and brick-layers" of your products. They will notice issues before they pose serious harm. Also, get closer to your customers. Salespeople are extremely important, but equally important are your customer service people. Listen to issues, complaints, and returns on products. Sort through the extremes but manage the issues before they become detrimental problems. The real money in a company is always made or lost at the point of production and the point-of-sale.

Task: Get out from behind your desk. Go talk with people whom you've never spoken with. Ask them honest and candid questions: What do they like about the product? Where do they see room for improvement? What do they hear from suppliers? From customers? Where do they see waste? Are there good ideas that haven't made it past their managers?

Lessons for Adversity

6. Understand the difference between inside problems and outside problems.

If a problem is with too much overhead, margins that are too low, or poor quality, these are examples of internal problems. If you're struggling with sales because customers are using different products or a service, this is an example of an outside problem. Inside problems can be fixed quickly and rather inexpensively. Outside problems are a bigger challenge and usually take more time and money to fix.

Task: Do a SWOT (Strengths, Weaknesses, Opportunities, Threats) analysis. Then divide issues into internal and external issues.

Lessons for Adversity

7. Create a detailed 13-week cash flow projection.

When facing adversity, your accounting statements from last month won't help you. Profit and loss statements are useless when trying to understand the future needs of your business. Only a detailed, rolling cash flow projection will help you understand how much cash you may or may not have in the coming months. Also, every week, you need to reconcile a budgeted projection against actual results. This will help you fine-tune your projections and stay on top of issues in a timely manner.

Task: Create a detailed 13-week cash flow (for an example, see appendices).

Lessons for Adversity

8. Beware of excess debt.

The immediate tendency of a business in trouble is to leverage assets and borrow more money. There are legitimate times when you need debt or equity to finance growth or perhaps to deal with a seasonal financing issue. However, once a company uses additional financing to resolve a cash shortfall without understanding the true nature of the problem, it will most likely become dependent on that habit and it will eventually run out of assets to leverage.

Task: Review the debt burden, the cost to service debt, and the debt ratio. What is an acceptable ratio to grow the company? Review senior vs. unsecured debt.

Lessons for Adversity

9. Do something to keep you moving forward.

Every day do something positive. The smallest of actions will still move you forward. Putting one foot after the other will get you to where you will need to be. You may not be able to control everything, but you can control some things—focus on those items first. Focus on tangible and measurable results.

Task: Make a list of things that you can do today that are positive. If you can't think of anything, start with the following: Smile and shake hands with all of the employees, talk with them, get their thoughts on how to improve, call all of the customers and thank them for their patronage, and call all suppliers and thank them for being part of the team. If you can't do that, go back to basics. Pick up a broom and start sweeping the shop floor. Pack boxes, put on shipping labels, take out the trash, organize the warehouse, etc. Remind yourself where you started. Be grateful each step of the way.

Lessons for Adversity

10. If you've decided that you've had enough at this point, understand the role of an investment banker.

There will be times when we have just had enough; we've done everything and it's not working out. Or maybe it's worked out and you've turned the corner again, but you're done. You're finished with the family business, with the industry, with waking up every day fighting for a dollar. If so, this is the point where you want to hire an investment banker. *Investment banker* is a strange and misleading title to most people who have never worked with one. They neither "invest" nor "bank." What do they do? They are sales agents for money or companies. They help sell, buy, or borrow money or companies. That being said, a great investment banker, like any great salesperson, can help you maximize the value of a sale of assets or the entire business. If they are great, then they are creative, have a lot of contacts, and move quickly. The problem is that many are *not* great. Many understand finance, and many are good at selling, but they generally chase too many deals and pass on projects to junior staff. Why? Regardless of the outcome, they get paid on a percentage of the sale (or loan, or investment). They obviously want to sell your company for the highest value because they will make more money. However, in a distressed situation, there's only so much effort they will put into the sale. You, as the industry expert, will have to work hard to help them understand the true value of the entire stakeholder chain (from suppliers to employees). There will be a tendency to focus only on cash flow and profits. If your company is distressed, those numbers won't add up to much. You will have to demonstrate value in the assets or a potential turnaround plan.

Also, there is a practice of trying to improve EBITDA (earnings before interest, tax, depreciation, and amortization) by showing Adjusted EBITDA numbers. Sometimes this is practical and useful. However, sometimes it's just fiction. Essentially, the investment banker puts together financial projections that include a lot of "if" statements. "If we cut overhead by 10%..." or "If we cut shipping time by 5%..." or "If we improve sales by 15%, the adjusted EBITDA will be $xxx,xxx." In other words, they're trying to sell a fixer-upper for a move-in ready price. This is okay; just be reasonable. You will turn away more potential buyers by trying to sell too much smoke than you would if you were honest and reasonable.

Task: Start interviewing investment bankers. Ask them for their experience in the industry, and samples of the Information Memorandums they prepared for each one of those clients. Review at least five of them. Then ask to speak with those clients. Try to find out their style of work. Mostly, try to find out if they delivered on what they promised.

CRISIS

C risis affects everyone differently. The typical response is either panic, freeze, hide, or attack. In my experience, none of these responses will take you to the place you need to be. If you panic, your mind will go to the worst possible outcome. If you freeze, no answer will come. If you hide, you're hoping that others will find the answer for you. And, if you attack without purpose and plan, you're confusing activity with productivity. What's the correct response?

Be calm. You need an open mind and patience to properly evaluate everything you are facing before you start making changes.

So, how do I deal with crisis on a daily basis, year after year?

Let's start with what happens on the days that I am not working, since they are so few. When I actually manage to get a day without any clients, I sleep. If I can't sleep, I find a way to escape into something completely mindless and menial. I'm looking for some remnant of innocence from my childhood. I look for popcorn, ice cream, and a walk in the park. Anything else—anything that resembles responsibility and adulthood—is just too much effort. Newspapers, bills, other adults—sorry, not today; it's just a day I need to pretend the world does not exist.

Vacations? I can plan them…I will even go on them…but I never enjoy them. I have been on the phone and my computer all day, every day, looking out my window at some of the most beautiful beaches, mountains, and cityscapes around the world. You can't ask a crisis to take a break. When you do this work, you are either in or you are out. There is no halfway or part-time measure.

So, what does 99% of my life look like when I'm working? It is a combination of juggling act, obstacle race, and emergency room. Something is falling, failing, or crashing at all times and I am racing to keep it in one piece before it and everything around it dies.

It is not uncommon to be overseeing multiple clients at one time. Often, I have been a chief executive of one company while advising other companies in crisis. Generally, we work in teams. I run my teams just like the military. There's a hierarchy and there's a structure. I need a lot of discipline and clarity within my organization or we would drown under the confusion and pressure from our clients. Our days are filled with dealing with one issue to the next. Aside from the usual graveyard humor, we don't have time for chitchat about sports, and weather. In my world, you get to the facts quickly or get out of my office. I'm not there to comfort you. If you want warm and fuzzy, find another job or buy a dog. I have empathy for people, but in a crisis, I know that if I don't move quickly, there will be no one around to care for. My primary concern is for taking care of the most amount of people; to do that, I need to accomplish a lot every day.

Most of my client engagements begin with this sentence: "We can't make payroll in three days; can you help us?"

It's always that dramatic and always that real. Sadly, many people do wait that long to make a call for help. It's not much different than people and their physical health. They change their bad habits only after they have had a heart attack or stroke.

My answer to the payroll question is always the same: "Sure," which is followed by, "I will send over my contract. When it is signed, and I receive the retainer, I will start, and you will have your payroll." Unlike an actual emergency room doctor, I need payment up front. I believe companies are living entities but they're not actually going to die right that moment. Knowing that these companies are already drowning in debt, it would be foolish of me to extend them any credit. If they can't make payroll, they have a long list of creditors, and I don't want to be one of them.

The moment the contract is signed, and the retainer is in my account, the first phone call is to their senior lender. It's generally a simple conversation. "I'm here. They've hired me. I need some time to get my arms around the situation. Can you release funds for payroll?" The answer is always, "Yes." The lenders have lost faith in the current owners and leaders of the business, but they have trust in me and my team. Why? Because most likely I have worked for them in the past, and hopefully I got their loan repaid in full. It's always about trust. If you have it, you have latitude to work. If you don't, you won't get far.

Once I have payroll, I have a few days to figure out what is actually happening at the company. My goal at this point is to turn days into weeks and then weeks into months. I know that if I can fix things to a point where I get "months" to work, then the chances for longer-term survival grow significantly. I'm never certain which way it will go. It might live or die, but in the meantime, I can pay off creditors, keep people employed, give suppliers time to find new customers, and keep money flowing through the economy.

I am always thinking about the long-term prospects for a company, but until a company is out of crisis the primary focus is on the short-term. We generally break a situation and company into smaller, digestible pieces. We'll start with the next two weeks, then the next 30 days and, finally, the next 13 weeks. If we can see what the next quarter looks like, then we'll move on to a longer period of time. In the meantime, the plan is to get through the day, every day.

As a crisis manager, each day begins with having to choose between bad and worse. I am never handed an easy problem. If it was easy, I wouldn't be there. There are always layers of complexity and competing interests for each decision that I make. I have scarce resources and little time. If I pay one person, another person can't get paid. If I fire people, others will be affected. If I only have enough product to ship to one customer, other customers will be delayed, and on and on. There's never a right answer. It is the fog of war. No two people will approach the issues in the same manner. Even after I have finished working with a client, I will analyze and second guess my decisions for years.

In the meantime, I have to find a way to evaluate and decide as quickly as possible. Generally, I don't have enough time to think through every option. Ultimately the only real choice that I have is whether to become cynical or to maintain some level of optimism. If I am cynical, my decisions begin to isolate and prepare for death. If I am optimistic, my decisions come with comments of support and hope.

My days usually start long before I am awake. Emails trickle in all through the night. Before I can wipe the sleep out of my eyes, I find myself staring at dozens of urgent or dire issues waiting for me to resolve them. I click through all of them, knowing that if I don't answer them, the cries for help will only get louder as the day proceeds.

In the next couple of hours as the rest of the world wakes up, my laptop boils faster than my blood pressure. In the middle of a crisis, it's not unusual to receive 60-100 emails per hour, every hour. I refer to it as "email snow." They come in so quickly that there is a cascade across my screen. I try to read as many of them as I can, deciding where I need to intervene and guide. In each case, I am careful to be clear; otherwise, the confusion will only compound exponentially, which will mean more emails. The goal is to shovel the snow faster than it comes down.

Generally, by the time I am finished reading the first round of urgent emails, my phone will start ringing. Bankers, lawyers, owners, other creditors, and random angry or concerned executives and customers are calling. Everyone wants something. There's always a list of demands and complaints. The demands always involve taking something from someone else, and the complaints are always against one another. I listen to everyone and I take notes of their issues. Then I try to manage their expectations while assisting them with their needs. This is probably the most difficult aspect of the job; taming the greed and anger. Everyone in and around this failing company feels as if they've been condemned to the beasts. They act as if they're in the Roman Coliseum fighting lions, tigers, and bears. In reality, they're fighting each other and they're acting like savage wildlife. If I can't calm this group and get them what they need, there's no chance of survival for the company. And in the end, everyone loses.

Crisis, by definition, is ugly. People panic. They fear losing their jobs, their homes, their social status, and their families. As human beings we crave stability. We need predictability. People in and around a business need to be able to accurately see and walk straight lines. In a crisis, as the leader, I have to try to remove the surprises. I need to bring reassurance and order, and words are not enough. The F yous and email snow are waiting for me every day. I have to literally and figuratively get my arms around a business in crisis and deal with each problem as fast as possible. If I don't, it will fall apart and no matter how hard I tried, in the end everyone will blame me, whether it's deserved or not.

By the time I make it to the office, I walk through the company and one by one I am confronted by employees. Some hate me and some cling to me. Most are confused by my presence. "Are you here to fire us?" "Are we going to make it?" "Should I be looking for a new job?" One by one and sometimes in groups I tell them the truth of that particular situation. There is always the temptation to lie and give a convenient answer, but I have never believed in that approach. I believe in building trust by being honest. To get through a crisis, I will need help from employees. They are the engine and creative force that will move a company. I will offer guidance, but the power will come from the employees' willingness to work through all of the chaos and change. Most are stunned when I first start speaking with them. Most never knew how bad the situation was. Most companies in deep trouble lied or hid the truth from their employees—it was just easier to live in denial. As I reveal the truth of their situation, the emotions pour out onto me. The messenger gets shot most of the time, and that's okay. They're in shock and they're frightened. Who am I to tell them to feel otherwise? In their eyes, I am just a stranger that showed up wielding a knife. To help them survive, I may have to slice through the company and change their entire working environment. Why shouldn't they be angry with me?

By the time I arrive at my desk, I take a break from the calls and emails and I move on to the next pile of misery and anguish—the stacks of lawsuits neatly arranged in one corner. Companies in crisis are under constant threat of litigation. Generally, before I start an engagement I ask, "How high is the pile of lawsuits?" They come from every direction; suppliers, customers, employees, lenders, and investors. Behind those lawsuits are dozens more that are mounting. Everyone wants the same thing—the one thing that I don't have—money. With lawsuits, I try to buy the one thing they don't want to give me—time. The discussion may be about right or wrong, but the real issues are time and money.

Every day, as I march through the barrage of issues and the onslaught of desperate people, the biggest challenge inside of me still is the battle between becoming cynical or remaining optimistic. The list of demands and confusion continues every day. Everyone is fighting. Everyone wants their money. Everyone wants me to find an answer to it. They don't want the *right* answer; they want *their* answer. They don't want it later; they want it *today*. They're tired. They're frustrated. They've been on this sinking and troubled ship for a long time and now they want out. The trouble didn't start when I arrived; it started long ago. They've been through months—even years—of anguish, confusion, and loss. In this type of environment people break. They get worn out. They change in a bad way. They become desperate and they cut corners. They turn on each other, and trust is hard to find. I am lied to every day. The days are filled with opinions and half-truths, and I spend a lot of energy trying to figure who is telling the truth and whose perspective is real.

I am surrounded by people who built the company. They've been there a long time. They were there when times were good—big parties, big bonuses. They claim to know what's wrong and how to fix it. But now times are bad, and they were the ones managing the company. They have to be wrong on some things, but they can't be wrong on *all* things because they helped build the company. The challenge is to figure out if what they're telling me is either right or wrong at the very same time that everyone else is yelling at me and threatening to sue me and fire me from the job.

Every day is a fight from all directions. I am there to save everyone, but they're overwhelmed with so much emotion they can only think in terms of anger and fear. They want all of this to go away, including me. It would be so easy to lash out at them or walk away. I could easily say, "The company should be liquidated." The reality is that whether I am saving a company or liquidating it, I bill the same rate. My fees don't change. As people and issues are raining down on me it would be easy to say, "Forget it. It's not worth it. Fire everyone. Shut it down. Sell off the assets and go home." But I don't.

In the middle of that ongoing battle between cynicism and optimism in my mind, I remind myself that I am there to save them from themselves. I have to keep moving forward.

By early afternoon, key employees and key customers find their way to me. They're good and they know it. They're loyal but they too have families. In their minds, I am a stranger at best. At worst, I am the enemy. Somehow, I have to earn their trust. I have to lay out the complete and honest picture from my perspective. And, hopefully, I have a path to take the company out from crisis and turn the situation around. If I do and they believe me, they will stay. If I don't and they're uncertain—if they are unable or unwilling to believe me, they will leave. One by one, as the best and brightest employees and key customers leave, the crisis will deepen. If this happens, the prospect for survival moves further away.

As I approach the end of a day, fatigue makes the debate in my mind between cynicism and optimism get louder. The constant nattering of negative, horrible, bad, and worse information starts to wear me down. "Can this work?" "Can we keep it together?" "Do we cut?" "How far do we cut?" "When do we cut?" "Where are the opportunities?" "Where haven't we looked?" "Should we sell everything?" "How long do we have before the company has melted down beyond the ability to pay its creditors?" "Should we just begin an orderly wind-down now?"

As this frenetic negative information reaches a boiling point, I then remember that I haven't eaten lunch. Often, I think that if I eat something I will see things differently. But, then I remember that when I am working nothing tastes good and I have a hard time getting food down. Usually by this point, I am exhausted, but I am nowhere near to being done. Another day has passed, and more problems are certain to have come up that haven't been brought to my attention yet.

Most likely, I will have at least one more conference call, usually with creditors and then with employees. I will review the most recent numbers; thousands and thousands of numbers. "Where is the cash?" "Are we burning cash?" "How much are we burning?" "Where's the fix?" "When will we be cash flow positive?" Over and over, line by line on countless spreadsheets. If one number is wrong, if one formula is misplaced, all credibility will be lost in "the numbers" and it will trigger another round of verbal abuse and calls for another meeting to review "the numbers." In a world of chaos, in a company filled with incompetency and inaccuracies, I have to find a way to make "the numbers" perfect. If not, the world will continue to spiral out of control.

As the evening begins, I resume shoveling of the snow on my computer screen. I answer emails, respond to problems, give directions, and answer calls for help.

When I manage to eat dinner, it's terrible. All sense of smell and taste have been deadened by the stress of the day. Nonetheless, I still eat. I try to pretend that I am enjoying the food and my surroundings. I watch other people smile and laugh. I watch them nod in approval as they listen to each other's stories, and I am exhausted. I know that even when I am successful, there will still be a long line of people who hate me. Try enjoying a meal with that thought in your mind.

By the time I lay down in bed, the entire day swirls around in my head and I continue to try to find answers for every issue and every person. I know that optimism is the path to creativity. It is the channel for inspiration and hope. Optimism is what will bring people together to help save and rebuild the company and the lives of countless people. Every day, this is the last thought that I try to hold in my head because I know that tomorrow the fear and panic will begin before I even rise.

I was interviewed by my next client while I was working as CRO for the automotive company. It was spring of 2008. Two gentlemen in their mid-50s appeared in my office, and they began by laughing at my Spartan environment. I had a modest office space with three rooms, including a meeting room and space for an assistant. It was located in a building built in 1929. Two-thirds of the building space lay vacant; it was quiet and mostly abandoned. I spent most of my time at clients' places of business, so I didn't feel the need to waste money on things for my ego. There were no pictures hanging on the wall. I didn't have an assistant. I had a coffee machine, but it wasn't plugged in. I had the same bottle in the water cooler for six months. I had a desk and electricity and the phones worked, and that was all I needed. My prospective clients sitting in front of me found all of this amusing. They thought I was cheap and certainly not successful. I found their giggling and musings sad.

Soberly I said, "Keep looking around. This is your first business lesson: spend money where it matters most to the customer. I'm a crisis manager. Do you care what your emergency room doctor looks like? The only thing that matters is that I can help you with your problems. So, what are they?"

That got their attention. Within a minute they told me that in a matter of two years they'd gone from being entirely debt-free to having every asset committed as collateral for loans. And, according to the company's balance sheet, they had lost their entire net worth, which was somewhere north of $30M. After an hourlong discussion, they changed their opinion of me and decided to hire me to conduct an independent assessment of all of their operations and managerial staff, hoping to construct a turnaround plan out from under this mountain of debt.

They were the fourth-generation owners of a 105-year-old furniture company. They principally made sofas and lounge chairs. Two years earlier, they had lost interest in running the company, so they appointed a trusted friend and longtime employee, the former CFO, to be the CEO. He was a nice man but a complete train wreck of a CEO. The company had been experiencing many operational problems for years. Rather than address and fix them, he just kept borrowing money to finance the losses. Eventually, he ran out of assets to sell or borrow against. The company continued to burn cash, but no one knew how to stop it.

As we conducted our assessment we discovered a severely bloated company. Years and years of existence had led to a sense of entitlement for many people. There were factories in five different states. In total they had 17 different legal corporations. They did everything from importing and manufacturing to retailing and franchising, and they even owned a lumber mill. There were 27 different bank accounts. There were secretaries for secretaries. Company-funded country club memberships were normal. The balance sheet included items such as "inside showroom." When I asked what that meant they explained to me that certain managers and certain members of the board had their entire homes furnished with custom-made furniture. They didn't buy the furniture; it was a benefit for their position. Every couple of years, they would refurnish. The bank, believing these were legitimate store showrooms, lent against the furniture as "current inventory." Everywhere we looked we found excess, and everyone had contributed to it.

Teamsters and steelworkers' unions had been at one

location since the '50s. They were tough. They had seen the owners' families make significant fortunes for decades; they never believed them if they told the workers "times were tough." The unions held to their work rules tightly. If a senior worker called out, a junior worker could not take his or her position—not even for the day. Only a person of equal and better experience could fill in. As a result of rules like this, production was painfully slow and behind schedule, which only served to put more pressure on cash.

We put together a turnaround plan that involved no magic or prayers. It was basic business. Consolidate under-utilized factories, cut all excess overhead, reduce SKUs significantly, focus on better margin offering, and manage to better accountability. The first stop was the unions. We asked them to help us with some concessions on benefits and make a few changes to work rules. It was a simple but solid plan. It would turn a $125k per week cash burn to a positive in 12 weeks. In a year, the owners would be well on their way to having their net worth re-established, in a leaner, cleaner, and faster company.

The owners didn't have the stomach to fire a few hundred people. Many employees already questioned their motives, and this wouldn't help, so the owners asked me if I would assume the CEO role for the duration of the turnaround plan. I agreed on one condition: that my team also had the COO and CFO roles. I wanted only my team, so we could work as fast as possible without any politics.

We presented this plan to the bank and the bank loved it. They claimed it was the most reasonable and achievable plan that they had seen in years. In the world of troubled loans, that was high praise.

We began the next day and moved quickly. In the first

week, we announced the closing of one plant, resulting in 400 layoffs. In that same week, I fired nine of the top 12 executives.

In the coming weeks, everything moved along as planned, until we hit a major roadblock. We discovered that we had $2 million worth of obsolete inventory. This inventory was listed on the books as current inventory and the bank was lending against it. There was no way this inventory was current. It tied into the design industry and it was at least five years out of fashion. I couldn't understand how this could have happened. The bank had auditors and the owners had their own independent auditors. How could two sets of auditors miss millions of dollars of inventory for years? When I looked into it, a conscientious employee explained to me that none of the auditors had ever been into the warehouse. They showed up every couple of months, but they always went to the local bar with the manager. Beer is a great distraction. Now, as CEO, I had inherited this problem.

There was no way I couldn't report this to the bank even though their auditors were apparently fine with it. I reported it and the bank barely paused to reflect on the fact that they helped create this problem. It was their auditors who had helped perpetuate a fraud for years. They could care less. They were one of the biggest banks in the country; they made the rules. Instead of finding an agreeable and gentle path around this problem, they simply decided to re-categorize the inventory and immediately remove $2 million from the borrowing base. Instead of rewarding my honesty, they punished me. Legally and technically they were correct, but they would have never known if I didn't bring them the information. I didn't expect them to keep lending at the current rate, but I did expect that we would work together to find a less dramatic way out of the situation. With a reduced borrowing base, I would not have enough cash to run the company. A challenging plan now became a crisis just because I had decided to be honest.

I put my sense of injustice aside because we quickly had to come up with a plan to deal with the immediate shortfall of cash. All of the assets were already secured by the bank. We couldn't liquidate any of them without dramatically shrinking the company. The only remaining answer was to cut. We had to make more cuts in staffing and we had to simultaneously cut everyone's pay. It was desperate, but we didn't have a choice. If we didn't, we wouldn't have enough cash for another week. So, we concluded that there would be more layoffs and a 7% cut in compensation across the board. As a gesture of good faith, I cut our firm's fees by 20%. But that gesture was almost irrelevant to thousands of people. We still had 1,300 employees, and fear continued to build as word spread that more layoffs and cuts in overhead were coming.

The next day, a crumpled note appeared on my desk. It read, "You won't make it to your car tonight." The director of Human Resources asked me if I wanted a security guard or police officer for the day. I knew people were frustrated and confused. This company had been part of the community for more than a hundred years. It had seen lean years but certainly nothing like this. The entire furniture industry had been under pressure for a long time. Many manufacturing plants had closed and their work was sent overseas. Now, thousands of people were fearful that this may be the very end of their company. For many of them across the country, there was no other option for employment. This was the end of the line. If the company closed, they would have to relocate and move their families to another city. They were scared and they were lashing out. I understood where they were coming from. They saw me as the undertaker that came to put the final nail in the coffin.

I looked at the director of Human Resources and said, "No. That's okay. I don't need security. I want them to look me in the eyes when they try to kill me." I had grown used to death threats. I knew people were angry and even dangerous, but I had a job to do. I had no time to bathe in their fear. I had to lead by example, with courage. My biggest concern was trying to figure out how I was going to raise $2 million to save the company.

We announced the cuts and I concurrently begged the bank to discuss a new agreement for the credit line. Without any additional assets in the company to borrow from, they needed to come from someplace else. The only place left that we could access in a hurry was from the owners. So, along with our new attorney, a sharp, strong, and quick-witted friend of mine, I negotiated a new deal that included a limited personal guarantee from the owners that would make up the difference in the shortfall of cash. They were relatively wealthy, but they had spent most of their money on things other than the business; namely, cars. Together, the two owners had 22 cars totaling several million in value. This was good news for me because they were assets I could borrow against to save the company. However, when the banker saw this on their personal financial statement he became furious. He didn't think that he should finance the company when the owners had millions in recreational vehicles. He changed his mind and now believed that the owners should sell the cars and inject the cash into the company instead of just offering a personal guarantee. He had a point, but we had already had a deal and we were out of time. The company desperately needed the cash. He didn't care. He backed out of the deal, then the owners became frightened and they too walked away from any other possible deal with the bank. Without the bank's additional funding, they were unwilling or unable to put more funds in.

We had a solid plan and we needed maybe seven more weeks to reach break-even. Everything was demonstrable and achievable. But here I was stuck in the middle of grown men acting like children. A few days earlier, everyone was in agreement. Now, because one banker had lost his temper and the owners were reluctant to part with their toys, this company would be killed. To this day, I don't understand why they didn't sell their cars in a hurry. And, similarly, I don't understand why the bank wouldn't accept them as collateral.

I pleaded with both sides. I begged them to be reasonable. I tried and tried. I just asked them to be practical and agree to the plan that they had previously agreed to. I wasn't asking for anything more. Operationally, nothing had changed. The company would hit its targets and return to profitability in a few months. Success for everyone was well within reach. But, I got nowhere. Everyone stopped listening to me. They threw a tantrum and hid in their offices sucking their thumbs. Each day passed, and cash ran dry. Within two weeks, I didn't have enough money to fulfill existing orders.

The banker, my former friend, stewed in his own arrogance and power as he watched the company's cash run short. Each day, he directed his subordinates to tighten the credit as our sales shrank. We were then unable to buy enough supplies to build any sofas and chairs for either existing or new orders. Without cash or credit, our sales eventually went to nil.

Unable to make or sell anything the bank had effectively killed the company. We had just enough money to make one final payroll. At this point, the bank then asked us for a meeting, on a Friday at 4 p.m. Our lawyers were present. My sharp-witted friend did all she could to try to persuade the bank and their attorneys. They were immovable. All we could do was listen carefully as the bank told us that they were pulling funding from us at the end of the day.

It was a legitimate company; there was a legitimate turnaround plan in place. We needed 60 more days and we would be well on our way to taking a negative $6M EBITDA to a $12M EBITDA—a great success. But we'd never get there, because at 5 p.m. we wouldn't have a bank. Without a bank, we couldn't pay employees, insurance, electricity, or anything. We would have to close all of the factories immediately, change the locks, hire security, and notify all of the local media and police in five different states. In a matter of a couple of hours, everyone would be out of a job and more than a hundred years of success would be killed.

I worked with my team late into the night making sure all of this was done. Around 11 p.m., I was the last one to leave. Mine was the last car in the parking lot. As a practice, I never parked in the "reserved" spots. I always parked at the back of a lot. It was a big lot, surrounded by cornfields. The next nearest neighbor was a plant approximately half a mile away. I stood at the door thinking about the note delivered to me a few weeks earlier. They were worried about a few more layoffs; imagine how they felt now that I had shut the entire company down. The employees didn't know all of the politics behind the scenes. They just knew that I was the new CEO.

There was no bravery in walking across that lot. I was just tired. I felt terrible and I wanted to go home. I got to my car in one piece. I had about an hour drive home, through mostly rural areas. I looked at my gas tank and noticed it was completely on "E." My mind was so preoccupied with saving the company that I forgot to put in gas. I knew there was a gas station about three miles down the road, so I would be okay. I drove there only to find out that it was closed. I was out of gas in a small town where I had just closed their oldest and most treasured company. Now, I worried that I was a dead man if an angry employee came across me stranded. I had no choice but to call 911. They sent a police cruiser. The police officer asked me for ID. He looked at it and he asked, "Are you the CEO of ABC company?" "Yes, sir," I replied. He then asked, "Are you going to be able to save it? I used to work there. It really is a good company." I said, "I'll try my best." They drove me to the next nearest gas station to buy a refillable container. Once filled, they drove me back to my car and wished me well. I had fully expected, at a minimum, to take a beating that night from disgruntled employees, but instead the universe sent me armed police officers. I'm not sure if it was a message from God but I was certainly grateful.

By the time I got home, my inbox was filled with more than a hundred emails from employees, suppliers, and customers all across the country. They contained questions, profanities, and terrible stories from people who didn't understand and didn't know how they were going to feed their families. I read every single one of them and I answered every single email. I tried my best to explain the situation in the most succinct way. I typed as fast as I could. Mostly, I just said, "I'm sorry. I'm trying. Don't lose hope." I was up all night.

The next morning, I gathered with my team and 25 employees. The bank let us keep five employees at each plant to liquidate the company. They asked me to draft a plan to sell all of the assets over the next couple of months and offered my firm $500,000 to oversee the liquidation. However, I had no intention of liquidating it. I was acting CEO. I only agreed to draft the liquidation plan so I could buy time to find options to keep the business alive. It was at that moment that I decided that I was going to fight back hard. I was not going to let this company fail. It had plenty of assets to cover the loan. There was no good reason it shouldn't have a credit line. And had we not found fraud with the inventory, we would have been seven weeks away from being cash-flow positive. This was a viable company.

In a matter of days, with the help of a friend of mine who was an investment banker, we were able to contact a few private equity and high-risk lenders that expressed interest in lending to the company. The investment banker was excellent. He was a finance dynamo who moved fast and knew how to work a difficult deal. By the end of the first week of the shutdown, we had a Letter of Intention to buy the debt from the bank from a legitimate private equity firm. The initial offer asked for a 3% discount on the entire loan. Within a few more days, we were able to secure two more offers to buy the existing banks' loan. The bank responded by saying it would take no discounts. That was understandable, but the interested parties were willing to negotiate on things like better advance rates on the inventory and other assets. For me and my team, this was all positive; the existing bank wanted out...and we had options for them.

However, the senior banker became even more petulant at this point. He just decided to stop talking with any of us. He refused to take calls from any potential investors or lenders. Didn't take calls from me, the owners, our investment banker, our lawyer. He just stomped his feet and told his minions to proceed with liquidating all assets across the country. Ten days passed and he refused to respond to any emails or phone calls. I knew that each day that we sat idle would make it that much more difficult to restart the company. I now was incensed at the stupidity and recklessness around me. I would not let this company die without trying everything possible to save it.

Facing no other options, I gathered my team from my firm and told them, "I'm going to set myself on fire." I was going to do the very one thing no one ever does in the turnaround business—go public. There is a spoken rule that everything stays in-house. The Special Assets department within banks; the place where troubled loans are managed is private and confidential because it is often messy and brings out the worst in people. No one wants their dirty laundry and mistakes aired out in public. Nonetheless, by this point, I had changed as a person and as a professional, I wasn't going to roll over. I wasn't going to stay quiet while I watched thousands of people lose their jobs because adult men were acting like selfish morons. I spoke with our attorney about what I was going to do and, God bless her, she thought I was nuts, but she supported my decision and even helped facilitate the next steps by giving me the name of a hard-hitting public relations firm.

I knew the moment that I hired them I was going to lose future business from this bank, other banks, and any law firms or investment bankers that heard about this. I would now be considered "untrustworthy." It was one thing to take on a major automotive manufacturer but quite another to take on a publicly traded bank. It was career suicide, but I chose to do it. I just knew that I wouldn't be able to live with myself if I let another company wither away, so I lit the match. I instructed the public relations firm to put as much pressure on the bank as they could, and they did. They were clever, honest, and fast. Press statements were disseminated around the country every other day.

It was an election year, so I called every congressman, senator, and governor in each state where we had manufacturing operations and asked them for help. My pitch to them was simple: "Help us save jobs and I will let you take all of the credit." All of them jumped in the mix. Politicians love great photo opportunities.

The union reps, now unemployed, asked how they could help, so I said, "Fill your pickup trucks with sofas and chairs. Bring them to the head bankers' office. Line the sidewalk with them. Then, simply tell him to answer his phone. Their eyes lit up. "We can do that." The next day they organized a caravan of two dozen trucks filled with our furniture. They drove to the banker's office and did exactly what I had suggested—lined the sidewalk with the sofas and chairs.

Before they left for this protest, I also gave the banker's personal cell phone number to the union and to a few thousand people across the country. So, as they protested they carried signs that read "Peter, Answer Your Phone" at the very same time that hundreds of people were calling him.

By this point, I was fully committed and there was no turning back. I then gave out the emails for all of the board members of the bank to the same few thousand people. I told them, "Send them your personal stories and pictures of your families. Tell them to tell Peter to "answer his phone." The unions and all the other employees jumped on it and took it even further. The next day, they organized a similar protest with sofas and chairs outside the corporate headquarters of the bank, which was located in another state.

Some thought that this was overkill, but I thought it was a measured response. I was just shedding light on the bank's actions. I just wanted a conversation, but the bank just wanted to liquidate a viable company. If they were going to act stupid and reckless, I wanted the entire world to know.

In response to all of this noise, the bank did what most big corporations do—they hid behind their lawyers. They responded by sending me a nasty letter threatening to sue my firm and me personally for defamation. My partners, naturally scared of entering litigation with one of the biggest banks in the country, wanted me to apologize and retract all of my statements. I had different thoughts. I was afraid of no one. I had done nothing other than tell the truth. I responded by saying, "Please sue me. I would like to go into court and explain to the judge how Peter is a child and the bank is closing a 105-year-old company when it is adequately secured in its loan. The bank is closing the company just because it can."

I then took it further. Not only did I not retract my statements, but I decided to shed even more light on the situation. I proceeded to give dozens of interviews to newspapers, TV stations, magazines, etc., across the country. I just kept talking and talking and talking. I knew eventually someone would start listening. In a matter of two weeks, working lockstep with the public relations firm resulted in hundreds of articles written across North America, and some even appeared in European publications. The *Wall Street*

Journal, Forbes, Businessweek, and *Bloomberg* all picked up the story. It was a true David and Goliath story; big, bad bank shutting down a treasured manufacturing company. Not surprisingly, the bank's stock dropped by 11% within two weeks.

The intense public pressure and the drop in the price of the stock pushed Peter's bosses over the edge. They told him plainly to "make the problem go away." We quickly arranged a meeting with Peter and the bank's lawyers. By the time we met, we had arranged several interested buyers that would invest new capital into the company. It took a few weeks and a bumpy road, but eventually we were able to restart the company. The company was sold to new owners. We couldn't get *all* of the jobs back, but we got a good portion back. The company is still around today and doing very well, just as it had done in the previous century.

As for me and my firm, the bank actively sent out messages that we were to be blackballed along with anyone associated with us. A lot of my friends had to distance themselves from me, but I understood. Big corporations—in particular, banks—like certainty. They like predictability. I was now officially "unpredictable."

When I set myself on fire, I burned a lot of relationships. Friends had to distance themselves from me. I knew they needed to protect their jobs and their families. I saved a company, but I paid a heavy price with regard to my credibility and career. The bank and their lawyers worked hard to paint a picture that I was crazy and could not be trusted. The irony of things: They wanted to sue me for being honest but now they were actively spreading lies about me.

For weeks, *Businessweek* had been working on this story. The journalist was terrific, and I shared everything with her.

By this time, I was already committed to being completely forthright. I explained to her that the banking world had changed dramatically, and very bad economic times were headed our way. Many bankers were acting like it was a depression. They were making extreme moves, calling loans and consolidating their own assets. I believed that situations like this were going to happen more frequently. The journalist told me that she was going to write an extended piece detailing all of my efforts to save this company. She was amazed at how far I went and that I was willing to throw years of my career out the window. I wasn't seeking the attention for me. I had just tried to help the company. But now, I was happy that this article would be published because it would help set the record straight. It would show that I hadn't lost my mind. That this was by design in an effort to help thousands of people.

She finished the article but then phoned me just before it went to print. She explained to me that her editor had decided to go in a different direction. He had decided to run a "power to the people" story; a story where the small-town mayor and employees came together to save this century-old company. In other words, he was just going to change all of the facts about how I had set myself on fire to save the company. How I had engineered the turnaround plan with my team; worked side by side with our diligent attorney and investment banker; led all of the communications with the public relations firm; solicited politicians, investors, and the media; fought the lawyers; and organized all of these people in a tremendous fight for life. He was just going to take all of that and erase it. Amazing.

I was disappointed but I still found it ironic and funny.

I chuckled and said to her, "You know that's not what happened."

She replied, "I know. I'm very sorry. But it's out of my hands. Thank you for all of your help." She hung up, and that's the story that went to print.

I spent all of my time trying to get to the truth of the company. I cut through lies and liars. But in the end, I was again wrapped up in more deceit. I went through all of that only to have it whitewashed in fiction. I shook my head and let it go. I wasn't looking for awards; I was just hoping for some honesty. Setting the record straight at that point in time just wasn't going to happen.

Nonetheless, I am eternally grateful to all of the people who played a role in saving that company. There were many, at all levels, across the country who helped. They are talented, they cared, and their desire to keep the company alive helped motivate me to lead the charge to the very end. What matters most is that the company is alive and doing well.

On a personally bright note, all of the press coverage started to attract new referral sources for me. The bridge to many of my old contacts had effectively been burned. But now, my phone would ring from new people. People who were interested in the street fighter; the guy who wasn't afraid to take on big banks and big automotive companies. It wasn't the reputation I was looking for, but I went with it.

Around this time, in the fall of 2008, the economic sky was actually falling. The stock markets were crashing, and the housing industry had slipped into a vortex. Once-jubilant bankers were now at a fever-pitch panic. Many of them had lost sense of all reason. Many more refused to accept what was happening, simply because they didn't understand what was actually happening.

Paul was CEO of a $200M residential home supplier with five different divisions in five different states. They made windows and doors for residential homes. His company was owned by a venture capital group of a major US bank. Banking laws prohibit a bank from lending to companies that they own, so another major US bank was its lender.

These two big banks had been fighting with each other for several months. Both were panicking as they watched revenues decline in this company, alongside the collapse of their own banks. The banks were crashing as fast as the housing markets. They needed to get out of loans to improve their own portfolios. They were experiencing tremendous losses in other parts of the bank, so they tried desperately and quickly to liquidate anything that appeared weak. In previous recessions banks were more patient, but this time was different. It was every man for himself.

Paul had been an accomplished CEO, but he too lived in denial of the rapid decline in his industry. He had helped build this company into an industry leader but was too slow to make adjustments when the revenue declined. It was a bit of arrogance, a bit of listening to his "gut" rather than facts, and a bit of greed. He and his bank believed they could sell the company for a sizable profit and dodge any trouble that may be coming. However, his biggest problem was that his lender no longer trusted him, his team, his financial projections, and his industry. They tried to schmooze, shuck and jive, bully, and negotiate their way around missing their projections for several quarters. Eventually, trust and time ran out on them. The bank was going to call the loan and shut them down if they didn't hire a chief restructuring officer to control the situation.

Late one night, Paul and his executive team called me. They had read about me in the papers and followed the last case I was on. They needed a CRO but they wanted someone who would be loyal and fight for their best interests. I explained to them that I had been fighting in every direction for more than a year and I needed a break. I needed some time to remember the good things in the world. They kept insisting that I start right away. They actually wanted me to start the next day. Finally, I relented and told them that I would send my team over to start the due diligence and I would show up in two weeks. They signed the contract that night and wire transferred a deposit for the engagement the next morning. This was the third company in crisis that I would be CEO or CRO for in less than 18 months.

My job was ostensibly to save the company and restructure it, just like my job title stated. However, my real job was to get my client (the first big bank) out of this deal they perceived to be cratering and to get the senior lender (the second big bank) out of this loan before the global economy completely collapsed.

My team worked quickly to find a way to reorganize this company to save more than a thousand jobs. It was only a few weeks before Thanksgiving. Losing your job and healthcare benefits in general is terrible, but losing them right before the holidays is just awful. This company made great products, and despite the greater economic considerations, it had reason to live. It was a market leader in many instances. With cooler heads and measured reasoning we should have been able to find a solution, but that wasn't the case. One set of bankers would yell into one ear, "Domenic, sell the damn company. It's worth easily what we paid for it. We should be able to clear $100M."

Then the other set of bankers would yell into the other ear, "Domenic, liquidate the damn company. There's $100M of assets. That should be more than enough to pay back our $60M loan."

They were both wrong. It couldn't be sold for a $100 million nor could it be liquidated in pieces for $60 million. The real answer was that these two reluctant lovebirds were stuck together and they needed to find a middle ground and weather the storm of the recession. But both of them refused to budge an inch from their respective position. They refused to even look at any plans we had drafted that would save the company. We had great employees, solid customers, and a steady supplier base. There was a core strength to the company, and as such we developed several viable operational restructuring plans that required just a little leeway from the owner and the bank. But the powers that be couldn't care less. I couldn't even get them to look at the plans. I pleaded with the bankers to give me 30 minutes to review options with them. They refused to even open the spreadsheets that I sent to them. They had their own worries, and this company was just a line item on one of their portfolio sheets. They needed to monetize this company because they needed the cash to bolster their bank's balance sheet.

The investment banker worked diligently to bring purchase offers to the table. Unfortunately, by this time in the economic cycle, only sharks were swimming in the waters. The best offer was $45M—far short of my client's expectations and very short on its ability to pay off the senior lender's credit line. I told both of them that this was the wrong route and offers would only get worse, but they only yelled louder.

As the purchase offers stagnated, the senior lender insisted that I draft a liquidation plan. He wanted an analysis from me on how long it would take to melt the entire company in order to get a full recovery of his loan.

A liquidation analysis is part science, part art. You are trying to calculate the value of your assets as you sell them. But it is not an ordinary sales environment. You have to strip away as many costs as possible, as fast as possible. Then, you need to sell your assets as quickly as possible without giving the appearance that you are desperate or your prices will plummet. At the same time, you have to try to collect outstanding receivables from customers and tell them that you can no longer supply them products. The moment you inform them of this decision, you lose a lot of leverage in your collection efforts. Many customers will hold out, hoping to renegotiate their invoices. Then in some cases, customers want you to make additional products for them so they can fill up their shelves buying them time to find a new supplier. In these circumstances, you need to figure out how to buy materials with dwindling cash reserves and make the product with a skeleton staff. So, when preparing a liquidation analysis, you have to take all of these highly questionable moving parts and make them as predictable as possible. When me and my team construct this type of analysis, we try to eliminate as many surprises as possible. We build the financial model brick by brick, line item by line item, double and triple validating the strategy.

As part of the process with this residential supply company, we called multiple real estate agents and equipment auctioneers. We spoke with customers about existing orders, and we evaluated collection rates on account receivables. The more calls we made, the bleaker the analysis became. No one wanted to sell industrial properties. No one wanted equipment and machinery—the warehouses and lots across the country were full from other failed companies. For many, the economic collapse had started a year earlier. It happened quietly but banks called many loans over the course of the year. As they liquidated companies they eventually ran out of potential buyers for all of these assets. When we actually did receive an offer, it was six to 10 cents on the dollar of book value. And existing customers, sensing blood in the water from what they heard in the rumor mill, gave cold responses to paying their bills. Any notion of an orderly wind-down slipped away. Everyone was fighting for their own lives.

When completed, our liquidation analysis showed that the lender would lose anywhere from $18M to $25M on a $60M loan if they forced an immediate shutdown of this business and a subsequent liquidation. The senior manager at the bank was incredulous. He refused to believe what we presented to him, despite the fact that we had worked with his bank extensively on other cases and he had previously trusted us.

"Domenic, there is absolutely NO WAY I will lose money in this liquidation. You're trying to tell me that those 100 trucks that were bought last year are now worth 20 cents on the dollar?"

"That's correct," I replied. "No one's buying them."

"Domenic—you're wrong. And, you're trying to tell me that this major retailer that has a $2 million receivable with us...you're telling me that I can't collect on that $2 million?"

"That's correct. We can collect, but if we shut down

this business they will have off-setting claims for business interruption. Those damages will be significant. This is one of the biggest home supply retailers in the country. These are the absolute wrong people to fight. They had been excellent customers and partners. Now, without warning, you are going to cut off their supply of product, which will affect their revenue numbers, and you don't expect them to fight back?"

"Domenic—you're wrong. We have better lawyers than they do. We'll get the money. I don't care what you say— you're just wrong. There's a hundred million in assets. We will liquidate this company and we will absolutely get our 60 million out. We'll get it in 90 days. I'm pulling the plug."

And, true to his word, a few days later, on Friday afternoon, they met with us, notified us of our defaults, and called the loan. Without a lender, we had to marshal all of the assets. Locks were changed on all of the buildings, security guards were put in place, public announcements were issued, and $200M of revenue was destroyed in an instant. Simultaneously, all employees were terminated—1,500 people were put out of work the week before Thanksgiving.

It was a disgusting display of arrogance and power. So easily, they cut the throats of thousands of people. They refused to consider any other options despite the fact that there was evidence that this path showed mass destruction for everyone. Their path was the worst path for all parties, but they were either too ignorant or too indifferent to acknowledge it.

Rather than listen to actual business operators, they handed the process over to their yellow bow-tied, overpriced lawyer. A diminutive man who wrung his hands with glee as he filled the bankruptcy budget with millions in fees for him and his firm. He knew this was a terrible path for the company and the bank, but he did nothing to advise his client otherwise. He was focused only on his fees. The bank couldn't for a minute consider changing its advance formulas on the loan for the existing assets so that the company could stay alive. Instead, in an instant, they decided that they could pay millions to their lawyers for truly unnecessary work. They couldn't even find it in themselves to keep the company open for six more weeks, until Thanksgiving and Christmas had passed. A simple gesture that would have eased the pain and suffering of thousands of people.

I showed them options where we could have kept the doors opened and not burned cash. There were options to move slower. There were several very reasonable and practical options. But they didn't care. They knew thousands of people for this company worked in small towns in five different states. They knew they would be instantly out of work and probably out of work for a long time. And they knew that hundreds of suppliers to the company would not be able to collect on their debt when they forced this shutdown. The moment it was shut, the value of the company declined precipitously. Millions of dollars that should have gone to operations and paying suppliers would instead be eaten up in legal and administrative fees in bankruptcy. Despite knowing all of this, they still said, "Shut it down."

The bank let me keep a shell group of employees to liquidate the assets for a short period of time before we officially filed for bankruptcy. It was the bare minimum I needed to do the work. I had approximately five at each plant. I still believed that there was value in the ongoing operations, so I embarked on a two-pronged strategy to try to monetize the assets and concurrently sell the companies.

If too much time passed, the value would be beyond repair. They would be viewed as dead assets. However, I knew that if we could sell the companies as fully-functional, going concerns, they could be restarted.

We worked aggressively with the investment banker to find buyers and re-engage previously interested parties. In the meantime, as we tried to sell smaller assets and collect receivables, we received a letter from the major retailer that owed us $2M. It read as follows,

> *Dear Sirs, our accounting shows that we do in fact owe two million for products purchased from your company. However, since we retail products purchased from you with a lifetime warranty and you will no longer be in business, based on the number of units we've sold over the past 10 years, we believe that there may be an additional twenty million in warranty claims. Therefore, by our records, you owe us eighteen million dollars. We will file this claim in court if we do not receive payment within thirty days.*

I sent a copy of the letter to the senior lender and suggested his "better" lawyers get right on it.

Concurrently, we didn't have a real problem selling off the new trucks because many of the employees had either stolen them or left them by the side of the road across the country. This happened because, in the bank's haste and rage, they had decided not to pay many employees' expense claims. Employees who worked on the road had travel expenses that had accrued and had not yet submitted those reports. I had prepared an estimate of these expenses, but the bank couldn't care less; they decided that it was not their obligation. There was $90,000 of accrued expenses owed to these employees but the bank wouldn't budge. They pulled the rug out from underneath the employees, but somehow they thought it wasn't their problem.

Imagine the situation from the employees' perspective. Without warning, they lose their job and their healthcare insurance and then they don't get their expenses reimbursed. People were angry. They lashed out and some stole things that belonged to the company to even the score. When I got word that cars, trucks, and materials were disappearing, I wasn't in a hurry to go find them. I thought it was a fair trade.

The greedy, paranoid, and arrogant bankers didn't stop there. They also decided that they should sweep all of the money in the health savings accounts—the money that belonged to employees.

The CFO had accounted for the employee's health savings accounts in a separate ledger, but he had not segregated the funds into a different account. By law, the bank had no obligation to see the funds as anything other than what was owed to them. So, in addition to firing everyone before the holidays, they decided to take the money that they had legally put aside for healthcare for themselves and their families. Even as chief restructuring officer, I had no recourse. The law was clear. The bank was acting in an immoral and evil manner, but they were not breaking any laws.

I protested to our lawyers and their lawyers and threatened to take the issue to the bankruptcy judge—but no one could find an actual law that was broken. The funds were supposed to have been physically separated into a different account. The total amount was $26,000. The bank was owed $60 million. Their yellow bow- tied lawyers were billing at more than $750 an hour. Juxtapose those amounts against $26,000 for employee healthcare. Money that employees had put aside for cancer meds, in vitro fertilization treatments, children's asthma. I looked into each employee's situation. They were hurting. They were now out of work, out of health insurance, and the money they had put aside had been stolen by the bank. I explored every possible option but the bank controlled all of the funds I used to run the company. I couldn't make a withdrawal or write a check without their approval. There was no legal way for me to return the money to these employees. It was frustrating and disgusting.

So, imagine: this bank, one of the largest in the country. Bright, shiny offices in New York, Chicago, Los Angeles, and other major metropolitan cities. At this exact time, in 2008, their executives are taking TARP money. They are being bailed out with federal funds. They are being handed a rescue net for their greed and stupidity. At that very moment while they are being handed a check for tens of billions, they are stealing from the healthcare savings account of these now unemployed people. If this wasn't a slaughterhouse, I don't know what is.

I was angry and bitter, but I knew that we had to continue moving forward as fast as possible.

Despite all of the ugliness and desperation, we were able to find buyers rather quickly. We were at the beginning of the Great Recession but we knew there was value in the company. We hustled to revive them before all life from them had dissipated. In the coming weeks, one by one we closed deals with several different buyers. One by one, we restarted companies. We closed one on Christmas Eve and another on New Year's. By the end of February, we had sold and restarted four of the five divisions. Sixty percent of the workforce was re-employed within three months of the original shutdown.

What happened to the banks? Big bank #1, my client, received zero dollars in proceeds from the sale of the companies. Big bank #2, the senior lender, lost $23M against a $60M loan…just as we had shown them in our analysis that they refused to believe. But hundreds of employees still have jobs, and hundreds of millions of dollars are still moving through the economy. If both banks had been more patient and more reasonable, none of this destruction and confusion needed to happen. The pressure of the economic crisis brought out the worst in many people. Fortunately, we were still able to find those who acted valiantly and help to rebuild through the storm.

Lessons for Crisis

1. Welcome to Special Assets.

If your business loan has moved into a department called "Special Assets" or the "Workout Department," it means that you are in a "special kind of trouble" and they want to "work you out of the bank." They are not your friends, but do not treat them as an enemy. Respect them and the process. They lent you money with the intent of getting it back. You've entered a gray zone of uncertainty and bankers don't like surprises. If you are here, that means they no longer trust upper management. Managers and the company have now become unpredictable. Your principal job now is to work as fast as possible to earn back the trust of the credit community by becoming predictably successful again.

Task: Introduce yourself to the workout banker. Try to meet face to face; if not in your place of business, at their office. Have pen and paper in hand. Ask them for a clear list of expectations—what they would like to see from you and when. If there is something unreasonable that they are demanding, voice your concern immediately. Don't argue; just try to come to mutually acceptable terms.

Lessons for Crisis

2. In business, cash is blood.

If the business is burning cash, you need to get to the heart of the matter quickly. Look everywhere. For example, in some cases, products are priced incorrectly. You may have to cancel or turn away orders, because selling them will cause greater cash loss. Offer one-time discounts on your receivables for early pay, sell off inventory, and explore every line item of your balance sheet to generate cash to help fund your turnaround plan.

Task: If you haven't created a 13-week cash flow projection, create one immediately. Determine the cash needs of the business as it is, then begin developing a plan to reduce overhead, which will improve the cash flow. Concurrently, figure out which assets can be liquidated or leveraged immediately to bring cash into the business to keep it alive.

Lessons for Crisis

3. Speed of the leader, speed of the group.

The leader sets the tone, pace, and expectations for the entire company. If the leader rises to the occasion, so will others. The first sacrifice should be made by the leader in every instance. If a leader is going to ask for skin from his/her employees, theirs should be cut first and deeper. If they're not up to the task, they need to move out of the way immediately.

Task: Make a list of things that you aren't doing but that you *should* be doing. Next, review all of the benefits that you and your family take out of the business—start cutting all of the things that are unnecessary to the survival of the business. The only thing that you need is a paycheck and healthcare insurance, and if you don't need a paycheck, don't take one. You only need a contract for $1 to have healthcare. Every available dollar should go toward saving the business. If you can't do that, prepare to sell it.

Lessons for Crisis

4. Create calm.

Understand at this stage that many people around the company are angry, confused, frustrated, and nervous. And, for the most part, these people are going to fight to protect their own interests. The notion of "for the greater good" or "for the good of the company" does exist, but the most noise will come from those who are fighting for their own best interests, which, in many cases, is natural and understood. They want to hold on to their power and their jobs. They want stability and security. Good employees will want to leave. Mediocre employees will want their jobs. Good customers will want to leave. New customers will be uncertain (having heard rumors in the marketplace). Suppliers will be stretched out and they will just want their invoices paid. Some will have already filed lawsuits. And your senior lenders and banks, sensing trouble, will start to reduce your credit lines at the precise time you need more cash. In short, pressure will mount from every direction, and everyone is mostly looking to take care of their own interests.

Businesses are living entities, even when they are dying. A gardener doesn't stand over his plants and yell at them to grow. A gardener plants, fertilizes, waters, nurturers, and pulls weeds daily. Calmly and earnestly he guides, and life grows. Creativity, strength, and endurance will all be fostered in a calm environment, even in the middle of a crisis.

Task: Review your attitude. Review the attitudes of key managers. Everyone is stressed, tired, frustrated, and angry. That is understandable but it's not productive. You need to get everyone to a place of calm and understanding. Calm but not aloof. You still need to move quickly to address the crisis.

Lessons for Crisis

5. There is some value in every business.

Even if on the surface the business appears to be losing money on many fronts, there is always something that can be made profitable. It's all about creativity and facts. Even in dead and dying industries, there is always one last supplier of that product or service...and they seemingly exist for a very long time. If there is money coming in through the front doors, then there is still a way to generate a profit.

Task: Around every troubled business there are many people who will say, "The business is crap. Close it down." And, often, the leadership responds with, "No, it's not. It's great." The reality is it's neither. There are parts of the business that are crap and parts that are great. You, as the leader, have to have the courage to gather your team, to find creative and productive ways to scale back the business, and start over. If you're burning cash and being pulled under by multiple forces, you can't hold on to everything at this point. Figure out what needs to go and cut it loose quickly.

Lessons for Crisis

6. You can make do with a lot less than you think.

When in trouble, go back to the beginning. Imagine the business as a start-up. How much money did you need when the business first started? What did you really need to get those first customers? What was really necessary? You didn't have millions for advertising. You didn't have millions for state-of-the art manufacturing. But somehow you found customers to buy your product or service. Go back to that time and build the business back up from a clean sheet of paper.

Task: Go back to basics. Make a list of all the things you had when you started the business. What is essential to the delivery of the product or service? What are the things that matter most to the customer? Save those and cut everything else, fast.

Lessons for Crisis

7. Romanticize nothing.

If your business has lost significant market share and margins, everyone is out to kill you. If your competitors don't put you out of business, inertia eventually will. Clean house—fast. Dump all of your old inventory, marginal products, and marginal employees. Sell off or donate all unproductive assets. Pour all energy and dollars into the products and services with the best contribution margins. Embrace the Pareto Principle; the 80/20 rule. Do the analysis and you will discover that most likely 80% of your revenue is coming from 20% of your products. Once you have that, dig into those numbers and discover where the best margins are—focus on building those segments. Oftentimes, troubled companies' top sellers are margin losers—which is one of the main reasons they are in trouble. They mistake revenue for profits. Their salespeople were beating their competitors because their product or service was underpriced. Sometimes, to survive, you have to dump your best seller (if you can't figure out how to make it more profitable).

Task: Conduct an 80/20 analysis of all of your product or service offerings.

Lessons for Crisis

8. Stabilize one thing at a time.

In a storm, secure one element, then build upon it. Imagine trying to put four pegs of a tent in at the same time in a hurricane. Put one in first, then the next, and so forth. Confidence and clarity will build with each secure element.

Task: You have your plan. Start by getting your arms around one thing, then move to the next. Don't do six things halfway; do one thing the right way and then move on. This will build confidence in your team and show progress to all of your stakeholders.

Lessons for Crisis

9. Respect your creditors.

Don't complain about your bank and their demands or about your suppliers. They lent you the money you needed—all they want is to be paid back. They don't want your home, your building, your assets—they want cash. And don't hide from your suppliers or lie to them. Be transparent and show them changes that you are making to get yourself out of trouble. If additional unforeseen problems arise—and they always do—let all of your creditors know. Don't brush the problems under the rug and risk having your creditors find out on their own. Understand that, at this point, everyone is staring at your company. The truth always comes to the surface. Be transparent and tell them how you will address and remedy the issue.

Task: Establish a weekly communication schedule with your creditors. It is possible that you may be talking with them daily because of your lending needs (borrowing base calculations, etc.). However, if you have your cash-flow projections updated weekly to measure budget vs. actual, then you should have a meeting or call with the lender to update them at this point. Concurrently, you can have a running list of action items that you are working on to turn the business around, and you should update them weekly on these items as well. Most importantly, don't avoid them. Bankers don't like surprises; they can handle trouble. If they know of the problem, they will try to manage around that risk. Work with them.

Lessons for Crisis

10. Under-promise, over-deliver.

No one expects a dying man to save the world. Every day, every week, work toward tangible and measurable improvements. It's important to remember that if you are at this stage, you've lost the trust of all of your stakeholders. You will have to earn back the trust by doing what you say you are going to do. No one will get excited about overly optimistic projections. You will impress them by staying alive and improving every week. Create a reasonable turnaround plan and stick to it.

Task: Review your projections and plan. Try to put them into three categories: worst case, realistic, and stretch goals. Make this clear to everyone. You can hope for the best, but you have to manage to reality and be prepared for the worst. It's okay to be in trouble; just don't try to hide it or deny it to your stakeholders. Honest, hard work, creative work, cooperation, and sometimes luck are the only ways out of this trouble.

DEATH

There is no obituary column or funeral for dead companies. A business can exist for years, decades, and even a century or more. Then one day it closes, everyone is fired, all the assets are sold off, and life goes on. Once in a while people talk about a plant closing or a long-gone retail store, but rarely do they take time to study what happened. In medical school, cadavers are used to teach future doctors. They dissect them piece by piece, studying what brought about their ultimate demise. And, in life, when someone close to us dies, we continue the grieving process by reminiscing about that lost life. We talk over and over about the good things and the bad things. We don't just bury them and never mention them again. Life carries on, but we try to make sense of life and the loss by examining it.

As human beings, as souls, we have learned over thousands of years that the closer we come to death the more we appreciate life. The entire process of being vulnerable and fragile is part of being alive. We fall, we get hurt, we go to doctors and hospitals, we have surgery, we take medicine, and despite our best efforts, we eventually die. It's messy, frustrating, heartbreaking, and painful, but we still need to see it, talk about it, and learn from it. That analysis and learning will only make us stronger as people and as a community. All of this applies to a business, as well. Often, it's the biggest living entity in a community.

We begin with the stark reality that, despite trying very hard, only a small percentage of all companies in crisis get saved. It's somewhere less than 20%. In bankruptcy, which is designed to shelter assets, it's even worse; less than 5% of all companies that file for Chapter 11 protection get to retain any equity at the outset of the case. These are staggering and oppressive numbers. The odds are always against us saving anything. With this in mind, I've learned to try to extend the life of a business and make the most of what I have in front of me. So, before I am the undertaker, I am often the hospice, and, just like hospice, the first introduction is a little off-putting until you get to know each other.

When I first walk into a severely troubled business I can smell death; it's terrible and it's inescapable. For years, I wondered if it was just me or if it was perhaps something spiritual. But after prolonged periods of living in crisis I realized it was an actual odor. It was stress. The senior managers and employees had been fighting and struggling and worrying for so long at such a high level of intensity that the stress was consuming them. After prolonged periods of extreme stress and crisis, your body chemistry changes. It's hard to run from it. It is disturbing, but it's a reality in the change from free-flowing life to the stagnation of death.

Not only do people change, but their environment changes as well. Divisions get closed, people get laid off, lunchrooms empty out, deliveries are less frequent, laughter is rare, and the hustle and vibrancy of a once thriving company is gone. The air gets heavy and starts to stink. It doesn't feel good to be in a building filled with ghosts. Pictures are faded, team-sponsored trophies are dusty, holiday parties are canceled, and bonus checks are a distant memory. Worse still, troubled companies are often found in towns that are an hour from nowhere. The company is filled with the air of death, but so is its community. There are vacant lots, "for rent" signs, empty billboards, and a handful of businesses hanging on. No one wants to move to these towns. Certainly no one wants to go work for a troubled company. The feeling of failure, isolation, and resignation to death permeates all levels in and around this business: the wrong industry, wrong technology, wrong location, too much debt, not enough revenue. Many times, it is dead and gone before I even get there.

Still, even in these situations, there is a way to find something positive. There is always a way to find a way to maximize the most from the assets and revenue that remain within the company. There is no formula for this type of situation. Every company is unique. Some situations require an immediate scale-back of 90% of all overhead while others require a well-orchestrated, orderly wind-down over a period of time. You have to be creative while being fully aware of all of the creditors' rights and interests. You have to accept that the business as it was is gone. Next you need to find a path to help pay back as many of the debts as possible.

As a crisis manager, I spend a lot of time dealing with the concept of "letting go." Helping people let go of their identities, titles, possessions, their status, their communities. Are all forms of death. When a person loses their job because a company is closing, all of these deaths accumulate within them and around them. As the senior manager, I am responsible for initiating all of that loss. I may not have created the situation, but it is my responsibility to resolve it, good or bad. The worst days were when we had to do mass layoffs or, in some cases, shut the entire company down abruptly. These were painful, miserable days. Only a soulless person could excuse themselves from the devastation that was being caused across thousands of lives that intermingled with this one, formerly living company. Every stakeholder, in and outside of the company, would feel some level of pain, despair, anger, and grief when a major division, plant, or the entire company was closed—including their families. Life would change for these thousands of people in an instant. All of that suffering would be brought into their homes and, in that instant, their family dynamics would change as well. Corporate genocide is real. When companies close, a ripple of death runs through entire communities.

And what happens to all of the debt when a company can't repay it? It goes away. On paper and in courtrooms, it's just erased. However, the real effect is that thousands of other peoples' lives are affected every time a line of debt is erased. That debt represents hours and material spent making a product or delivering a service. Somewhere along the line, others paid for that line of debt. When it's gone, they pay for it again. Their business will be affected. Someone may lose their job. If they get strapped, then their debts can't get paid, and so on and so forth.

Bankruptcy was created to protect creditors. It is a legal vehicle to stop the further decline of a business and shelter the remaining assets. A Chapter 11 filing is called "Debtor in Possession." It gives the appearance that the debtor is in control and has time to restructure the company so that he or she can pay off the company's debts. The reality is the debtor still has legal authority over his or her company but he or she is not in control.

The senior lenders or senior creditors have all of the

power and control. They are generally the ones who force a Chapter 11 filing. They do this as a vehicle to collect their debt. They are first in line; they see a declining situation, so they say, "We need a time-out and a plan to get us back our money." In general, this means there is a sale of those assets where the senior lender gets all or most of their money repaid. Rarely is there any money for all of the unsecured creditors. The unsecured pool is mostly hundreds— sometimes thousands—of suppliers to the company. They are left hunting for scraps that, if found, are eaten up by lawyers' and consultants' fees.

Bankruptcy does help save some value and protect some jobs. However, having seen both in-court restructurings and out-of-court restructurings, my preference is to stay out of the legal system. If you can find reasonable people and you can work quickly, more money will be distributed to all creditors along the food chain. Once a company files with the court, a great portion of the money that could be used to fix the company gets used up in professional fees. Lawyers, accountants, consultants, and court administrators all stand in line before unsecured creditors.

Having experienced all of this waste, I learned how to keep a company alive and limping along for an extended period. Why? To stave off death. My belief is that if money is coming into the front door, it shouldn't be closed. I believe in keeping the company open as long as there is positive cash flow, even if there are massive debts that have been accumulated. Each day a company has positive cash flow is another opportunity to help pay off creditors. Many times, those creditors are hundreds of other small businesses. They sold a product or service, and now they just want to be paid. Every dollar counts.

And, as long as the company is limping along, people remain employed. A paycheck is a paycheck. Keeping the doors open keeps money flowing to some employees and gives them time to look for a new job.

When a company finally does reach its end, you close the doors and try to sell off everything conceivable. Even in death, there can be value in a business.

One year into the Great Recession, I was hired to help a regional retailer that was owned in a trust by all of the employees. The company needed to hire me after they received a letter from its bank stating that they would not be renewing the credit line to them in the coming year. It was the fall of 2009. Most of the banks had taken significant write-downs in their portfolio. The troubled loans departments in all of the banks across the country were overwhelmed with problem companies. Credit had tightened. So, when they could easily get out of a situation, they did.

This retailer sold school supplies to elementary and high school teachers. It was a seasonal industry; once a year they needed to draw heavily on a credit line to build up their inventory when teachers prepared for the beginning of the school year. Without a credit line, they would have to shut the doors.

The company had been in business for more than 40 years. It was two weeks before Thanksgiving and despite this horrible news from the bank, I refused to lay off a few hundred people before the holidays. Life was hard enough without having to go into the holidays without a paycheck, health insurance, or even prospects for a new job.

We conducted a quick assessment and concluded that the company was a financial and operational disaster. Even if we could fix everything internally, external challenges were even more difficult to resolve. Competitors in the same industry had far surpassed this company in terms of product offering and service. As such it was very difficult to construct a turnaround plan without a significant injection of cash and talent. I knew that we could eventually find better managers, but getting a new bank or new investor would be virtually impossible. These were significant obstacles but that didn't mean we were dead in the water. I knew there had to be another option. We might not be able to turn it around but maybe we could offer some form of corporate hospice.

Sam, the CEO of this retailer, was a handful. He managed to do almost everything wrong and make almost everyone he met angry at him. He turned an $80M retail school supply company into a $20M company in less than five years. Sales, marketing, finance, operations, employee morale, and customer relations were all suffering terribly. There were 270 employees still hanging on. They were miserable, but they needed the job. There was nowhere else to turn in the middle of the harsh economic environment.

The CEO had done many things wrong, but he managed to do one thing right; he paid his suppliers on time. For some reason, he was very efficient at paying all of his suppliers within 30 days. For us, this was an opportunity to generate some cash. We concluded that if we could convince all of the major suppliers to give us 60 days to pay our bills, we could have enough cash flow to finance us for an extended period of time. We put together a 13-week cash flow with this premise and with other operational improvements as assumptions, and we showed it was possible to survive without a new credit line from the bank. There would be weeks that we would have less than $200 in the bank account, but in my eyes, it was more than zero, so it worked.

The pitch to suppliers was simple: "If you give us 30 more days to pay, you will still have a customer. If not, we're out of business in a couple days."

The majority of suppliers signed on. They became our credit line. At the same time, we put in place a couple of dozen changes at every level. We were able to keep this company alive and hundreds of employees working for another 10 months. Ten months without a bank. Ten months that kept millions moving through the economy and giving many people a little more wind to get their next job. It wasn't perfect but many times, it doesn't have to be; you just try to stay alive as long as you can.

Of course, as in life, not all deaths are similar. Not all die peacefully in their sleep; many go out kicking and screaming, and a few try to take as much as they can with them to the other side. In these situations, there is no ambiguity in my role. I am the heavy. I am there solely to protect assets. In these cases, most of the employees are gone and the business is finished. It's just about minimizing the damage that was already caused.

In one particular instance, a bank in NYC was struggling with a complicated loan. They had made a loan to a movie storage business. The bank's lawyers told them not to take the movies as collateral because if they were damaged or went missing, it could cost them much more than the actual loan. This business stored thousands of movies underground in cold storage. They stored safety videos for automotive companies and they also stored movies for all of the big Hollywood production companies. This storage facility also did movie restoration. It housed some very high-profile movies. Most notably, Martin Scorsese had a movie restored here. So, in an effort to avoid greater liability, the bank only took the account receivables as collateral.

This company was now in bankruptcy. A forensic accountant for the bank had determined that the $10M of receivables listed on the balance sheet were only worth $800k. It was his conclusion that the owner, Jack, had created a work of fiction with this balance sheet. In some cases, customers owed him money and he would cut side deals with them. They would do work for him on other projects or investments and he would extinguish their debt, which would have been fine except for the fact that Jack never removed the debt from the books. Instead, he represented it to the bank as perfectly collectible receivables. In other instances, Jack just made up the customers. They didn't exist. He just wrote in a number for the receivable.

The bank had been defrauded and now they were trying to minimize their write-off. However, after months of trying to collect the debt in a bankruptcy proceeding, not one penny had been recouped. Jack made it as difficult as possible for them to return the movies to customers, so they couldn't collect the receivables. The bank was terrified to have a trustee appointed to the case or to have any representative handle the movies. Their lawyers kept advising them that the liability was still too great. Word had spread that some employees had stolen movies in lieu of receiving their last paycheck so there was also an expectation that someone would have to pay for these missing movies.

Jack, like many criminals, knew how to exploit weaknesses and insecurities. For months he had been lying, manipulating, and threatening everyone in the case. A judge typically would not tolerate this behavior, but Jack was a great manipulator. He kept providing perfect excuses for not returning any movies. He fired the storage managers and told the judge they were stealing. He also fired his entire IT department and told the judge that the system was broken. Systemically, he fired everyone so that he was the only person who could do anything. Then he told the judge that it was just too much for him to do but he had no choice because everyone else was untrustworthy.

The banker in NYC had kept me apprised of what was happening. It was early in my career. I had only been in the crisis management industry a couple years but I knew this was the wrong approach. All along I had told him to ignore the lawyers and just get in there and ship the movies back to customers. I told him that Jack was playing games hoping to exhaust everyone so that he could hold on to his company. He hoped that people would get tired and walk away from their debts. He also knew that once the movies were returned, he would possibly be facing a criminal trial. After five months of inaction, the banker finally decided to hire me.

The company was located a couple of hours away from my principal office in the Midwest. When I arrived at our scheduled 8 a.m. meeting, there was a big, empty gravel parking lot that was large enough to fit 200 cars. There was only one car in the lot at the time, however, and I parked next to it. I walked into a large, old building that was dark and smelled damp and stale. There was no one within sight. I began walking down the hallway when a portly man came out of a room. He smiled and said, "Oh, hi. I'm Jack. Follow me."

I followed him into an adjacent meeting room with a table big enough to seat 12 people. In the middle of the table was a large tray of fresh donuts and a pot of freshly brewed coffee.

I thought that was interesting—it was certainly hospitable. I wondered if others would be joining us. Jack offered me a donut and coffee. I took coffee but declined the donut; I didn't want glaze or powder on my chin for this conversation. Jack sat at the head of the table and I sat in the middle along one side. Before I could take my first sip he started a prologue.

"Thank you for coming but the bank is really wasting your time and my time, and quite frankly, my money and their money. I don't know why you are here. There's nothing that you can do and nothing that I can do. The bank knows this. I've explained everything to the court. Everyone knows this. So, I think you should just go."

I found this amusing. I smiled and said, "Sure, Jack. I understand. I don't want to waste your time or money. I just need the inventory list and then I can go."

His tone and demeanor changed quickly. He was no longer the jovial host with donuts. He started to channel Archie Bunker.

"Boy, you really are some kind of idiot. I thought the bank was sending someone smart but you're an absolute moron. I'm going to call them and tell them not to pay you. You're just a fucking idiot. There is no list. I told you; the entire system is down and there's no way to get it until it's fixed. Now, will you just get out of here?"

I smiled again and said, "Jack, I just need the list. I know there's an inventory list somewhere. I'll even take an old one. I'm certain it hasn't changed much. I don't need a system or a disc. I just need a paper copy."

He stared at me with dark pupils and started turning purple. He turned around and moved his suit jacket off the back of his chair. I saw a gun in a holster hanging on the chair.

He pulled out the gun, pointed it at me, and said, "I told you to go. So go."

I knew I was outmatched, and I knew he was desperate and clearly crazy. I also knew that there was no one else around to even hear a gunshot. I stood up slowly and said, "No problem, Jack. I'm going. Sorry to bother you. Thanks for the coffee."

I walked out hoping I wouldn't be shot in the back. But by the time I got into my car and got to the end of the parking lot, I was angry. It was October 2001. It was six weeks after 9/11. The wounds and trauma from that horrible event were still fresh. I had many friends and a close cousin who had worked in the towers and financial district. The previous two years, I had travelled to NYC approximately once a month. Routinely, I had meetings with bankers or lawyers in and around the towers. I had just been there in August. In the financial industry, all of us knew someone who had perished in that heinous attack.

Like many, at times, I felt powerless at the sight of those buildings falling. The image constantly replayed in my mind like a nightmare I couldn't shake. It surprised me. It stunned me. And now I wanted to do something about it. I couldn't fight terrorists but I could certainly fight this degenerate scumbag who had just pulled a gun on me. I had had enough of criminals bullying people. This time, the bad guy wasn't going to get away with the crime.

I called the banker in NYC and told him what had happened. He was mortified and apologized incessantly. I told him, "No, really—it's fine. I'm going back in there. I will get you your money." He thought that I was suffering from shock. He couldn't believe that I wanted to go back in after a guy had just pointed a gun at me. I told him, "No problem.

Let me take care of everything. You just call his lawyer and tell him that we want to meet again tomorrow at 8 a.m."

I met with the bank's lawyers and asked them for help in hiring an off-duty cop to come with us to the meeting. I also requested an additional colleague of mine to attend as well as the forensic accountant.

The next morning, I stood in the parking lot waiting for the others. A white sedan with completely blacked out windows raced through the gravel kicking up dust. As the car neared, I read the license plate: "No Bail." The car parked and out came a guy, 6'2", brush cut, wearing gold-tinted sunglasses, tight jeans, and a black polo shirt, and holstering a 9mm on his right hip. I thought to myself, *Perfect.*

The off-duty police officer asked, "Sir, what would you like me to do today?"

I nodded my head and said, "You stand right next to me at all times. If the portly, bald, sweaty guy so much as threatens or tries to harm me, put a bullet in the middle of his head."

Without missing a beat or asking for clarification, the cop said, "Yes, sir."

We entered the room with the others. Again, there was a generous tray of donuts and a pot of freshly brewed coffee. Seated around the table was the forensic accountant, my colleague, the bank's lawyer, Jack's lawyer, and Jack, once again at the head of the table with the same suit jacket draped over his chair.

His lawyer immediately asked, "What's with the heat?"

"As you are well aware," I replied, "your client pulled a gun on me yesterday. I think that he is unstable and dangerous. So long as he behaves today, he won't be killed." Of course, being a criminal, Jack denied the entire incident because there were no witnesses.

His lawyer then said, "I think this is all an over-reaction. Jack is a good person. We can have the police officer wait in the other room."

I smiled and said, "No, thanks. He'll stand right next to me until we get the inventory list."

As soon as I said the word "list," blood started to rush into Jack's face. It was at this point that he started to call me different names. Somehow, he forgot my name from the day before.

"Fernando, I explained to you yesterday that there is no list, and none could be generated."

I'm not sure why he called me Fernando, but I didn't want to correct him. My intent was to make him explode even worse than the day before. I was either going to get the list or get him permanently removed from the premises by showing everyone what a lunatic he was. I hadn't shared my plan with anyone else, though. I needed authenticity for what came next.

I said, "Well, Jack. I don't know. I think there's a difference of opinion. I think we should review the forensic accountant's report and then get everyone's thoughts."

Jack steamed. I knew that the only thing worse than wasting his time would be wasting his money. I also knew that the cost of the bankruptcy was being shared between him and the bank. As assets were liquidated, his half would go to pay all of the costs. So, when I filled this room with people, I knew that Jack would be counting the dollars. Everyone but him was on an hourly rate, including the cop giving him a death stare. As the accountant spoke, Jack became restless. Everyone had heard this report; he would wonder why it was being read again.

Suddenly, Jack jumped in. "This is ridiculous. Why are we doing this? Everyone should just go home."

I said, "We'd love to, Jack, as soon as we get the list. I know there's a list somewhere. How did you run a business without an inventory list? I thought this was a good business. Good businesses know where their inventory is."

And there it was. Just as I expected, Jack blew up. He turned purple, smashed both of his fists on the table, stood up, pointed his finger at me, and started to spew, "You're an imbecile. You're an absolute fucking idiot. You have no idea what you're doing. You're a piece of shit. Get the fuck out of my building." Then, he took his own advice and stormed out of the room. I looked around the room at the others as if to say, "I told you so." His lawyer went after him and he too left the room. After 10 minutes, Jack calmed down and returned to the table.

Everyone looked at me for the next step. His lawyer asked, "What's your next question?"

I lowered my head, softened my voice, and replied, "I would like an apology."

My lawyer turned to me and shrugged his shoulders, and Jack's lawyer asked, "For what?"

"For calling me names and using profanity. That's not nice. I've been polite and professional. Why can't he be the same?"

"His lawyer looked at me and said, "You've got to be kidding me. Grow some thick skin."

I replied, "Would you talk like this to the judge? Maybe we should have this meeting in the courtroom. I'm asking for the same level of discourse that we would have there."

Sincerely, I couldn't have cared less what he called me. I had been called much worse. I just wanted to change the pace so I could make him my personal squeeze box. In and out, in and out. I knew eventually, he'd bust.

Everyone nodded and then understood that it was a reasonable request. Jack sheepishly said, "I'm sorry for yelling, Ferdinand."

Amused that he had changed my name again, I replied, "That's okay, Jack. I know you mean well…So, let's resume. Where's the list?"

In a flash, his face turned purple, both fists slammed the table, and he proceeded to call me and my family all kinds of awful things. He laced a three-minute rant with rancid profanity. Then he stormed out of the room again. This went on for two hours: swearing, storming out, and then apologizing to Fernando or Ferdinand.

I was intent on keeping everyone there all day, so I kept asking question after question about the inventory. At one point, he stood up and began pointing his finger at me and yelling, "You idiot. You stupid fucking idiot. Why would the bank pay you $250 an hour? You're shit. You're not worth a dime. Stop wasting my money. Please go home."

I waited until he sat back down. Then I took a long pause, lowered my voice, and with a tinge of sheepishness I said, "Umm, Jack? I don't make $250 an hour."

Jack looked at me in confusion.

I continued, "My colleague makes $250 an hour. I make $300."

I think that one finally sent him over the edge. He wanted to kill me. No words came out of his mouth. He just turned purple and smashed the table with both fists four times. *Bang, bang, bang, bang!* Then at the top of his lungs he yelled "FUCKER!" And, once again, he stormed out of the room.

I am convinced that had I not had the police officer there, he would have come after me with his gun.

As we approached the third hour, I asked for a tour of the facility. As we toured the warehouse I saw numbers at the end of each aisle, similar to numbers at the library. I pointed to these numbers and asked, "Jack, what are these?"

He rolled his eyes and said, "Boy, you really are stupid. You don't know the first thing about business. You moron. The numbers are for the list so we can find the movies when a customer asks for them. You idiot."

Bingo. Had what I needed.

I looked at his lawyer and said, "He just admitted that there's a list in front of all of these people. Go get it or we call the judge right now." Jack was devastated but his lawyer compelled him to comply. The list showed up in 10 minutes.

Jack's shenanigans didn't end there.

About a week later, on the first day that we tried to ship out product, Jack decided to lay down in front of the delivery truck in the driveway. I was not on site but my colleague was. Not knowing what to do, he called me in a panic.

I told him to walk over to Jack, put the phone near him, and put it on speakerphone. He walked over, and the truck driver joined him. They stood by Jack, holding the phone so he could hear it. I then yelled into the phone, "RUN HIM OVER."

My colleague was stunned. He asked, "What? Are you crazy?"

I then yelled, "MAKE HIS BIG PURPLE HEAD PART OF THE PAVEMENT," and I hung up.

Apparently, the truck driver smiled and got back into his truck and revved up the engine. He too hated Jack.

I was determined to show Jack that I would go further

than he ever would. It didn't take him long after that call to make him move out of the way.

Shortly thereafter he wrote a 27-page letter to the judge complaining that Ferdinand and Fernando were destroying his business. It took the judge a while to figure out that I was the "Spanish Destroyer."

In less than two months we returned most of the movies and collected the receivables. We hired former plant managers who had been fired by Jack to help us find all of the hidden and mislabeled inventory. We found a lot more than the forensics had shown. The bank was able to be repaid in full, and the remainder of the business was liquidated for the benefit of the unsecured creditors.

As for Jack, he went to jail sometime later.

This is death in a business. It's during these last moments that sometimes the most colorful and ugly aspects of humanity come out. People are desperate to hang on to an identity, cash flow, or just someplace to go. They spent so much of their life trying to get things that they haven't learned to let go. They can't grasp the concept of exiting a business gracefully and honorably. This is exactly what happened to my client named Bob.

Bob really liked being CEO. He liked having a wife and kids close to his business. He also liked having a mistress in another city, close to that particular location of the business. He especially liked having yet another girlfriend, out of state, close to another division of his business.

Bob was always very busy. He had four cell phones: one for the car, one for the boat, one for the cottage, and one just in case the others didn't work. Apparently, he hadn't grasped the concept that cell phones were *mobile* phones.

He visited each office and girlfriend on a weekly basis.

He missed most of the meetings, but he swore he was in attendance. He had an assistant in each city and a great office to match. He never answered emails, but his assistants were always polite.

Bob had a good life. He had inherited his father's auto parts distribution business. He also inherited many government contracts. He supplied countless parts for police cars, school buses, city buses, and municipal trucks. His father and the business had a lot of goodwill in several different states.

Then, one day, Bob got a call from his CFO. Apparently, no one had noticed or cared to tell anyone that the company's credit line was maxed out and that the company had been bleeding cash for the past year. Bob just figured everything was as fine as it always had been. His credit cards and cell phones worked; other than that, he didn't see any issues.

As he was both absent and absentminded, Bob hadn't noticed that his inventory had been shrinking. (*Shrinking* is just sometimes a polite word for "employees stealing products.") It's sometimes difficult to notice shrinkage when you have thousands of tiny parts.

He also didn't notice that his gross profit margins were shrinking. He didn't want to share detailed financial information with his staff, so none of them knew or understood the concept of contribution margin. As such, his sales team was incentivized on revenue alone. Unchecked, they just kept selling at whatever price the customer thought was reasonable. It didn't matter that they were now selling 30% of their products at zero or negative contribution margin.

Not overly worried, Bob called the bank and asked if the credit line could be extended. His father had banked there for years, so he figured it shouldn't be a big deal. It was just "a bump in the road."

The banker agreed to additional credit; however, he just needed a little more collateral to secure the loan. Bob again thought, *No problem. Just a bump in the road.* So, he signed over new assets. Then he called a meeting with his senior managers and asked them what was happening. They responded with a few well-sounding but meaningless answers:

> *The pipeline is full. We're just waiting for signatures. We're on it.*
>
> *The government is doing some belt tightening, but we'll be okay. We're top of the list.*
>
> *The economy is a bit slow, but they're telling us that their cap ex budget will be bigger next quarter. We're good.*

Those were good enough answers for Bob, so he resumed his busy life. Within three months, however, his additional credit line had maxed out and the decline of his company accelerated.

At this point, his banker called him to inform that soon they would be liquidating the additional collateral he had provided. Bob was stunned. How could this be? Why so quickly?

In his haste, Bob had pledged the family trust as collateral. The trust was comprised of 100% of publicly traded stock. The loan agreement stated that when the average stock values in the portfolio reached 85% of the loan value, they would be immediately liquidated; in this case, dissolving his family trust. Unlike buildings and machinery, stocks can be sold with a phone call and the push of a button. The stock market was in a correction and the lender had no choice but to sell the stocks if they hit that valuation.

By the time I arrived at the company, Bob had run out of options, so we had to move quickly. He had no additional collateral to post or replace his family trust; everything else was maxed out on mortgages. There wasn't enough time to fix his company, if it even *could* be fixed. His mother and sister were dependent on that trust. If it was liquidated, the entire family would be left with nothing but a badly damaged and declining business.

The best option was to sell the business to a competitor. That would be the fastest way to generate enough cash to hopefully cover the bank debt. A financial investor would take too long to get up to speed on the business and industry. A strategic investor, on the other hand, could move through the assets and customer base, quickly deciding what they needed and what it was worth.

Within a couple of days, we had an interested buyer and a signed nondisclosure agreement. Within a week, we had a reasonable letter of intent and an asset purchase agreement was drafted. The buyer would be able to close the transaction within a few days, and he would even absorb some of the employees with the acquisition. The business was only partially saved, but we had avoided a meltdown, which was excellent. The night before closing, however, I received a phone call from the buyer.

"Domenic, you better get down here right away. I am walking away from this deal. I'm done."

Apparently, his auditors had decided to do some last-minute, late-night work. And so had Bob.

Disgruntled, angry, and faced with the prospect of losing his steady paycheck, his boat, the cottage, at least three cell phones, and perhaps his mistress, his girlfriend, and his wife, Bob was acting desperate and stupid. After the sale, he and his family would still have the trust, but he wouldn't have much of anything else to support his busy lifestyle. So, Bob decided to renegotiate the asset purchase agreement. He had just forgotten to include anyone else in those discussions.

Bob rented several trucks and got a couple of soon-to-be former employees to help load a few pieces of machinery. He didn't think this was stealing because he believed that he still owned them. Of course, he had no intention of removing them from the list of assets attached to the agreement. He figured if they noticed, he would plead ignorance and file an insurance claim for the "stolen" equipment.

I drove to the company that night and I let the buyer vent. I agreed with him that my client was a lying, philandering, incompetent manager and a thief. But that was irrelevant to all of the thousands of parts that he was buying, not to mention having an easier and clearer pathway to new customers and more government contracts now that this business would be liquidated.

He agreed. We removed the "stolen" equipment from the sale price and the deal closed the next day. The bank was paid in full.

The family business evaporated but the trust was preserved.

Bob disappeared into the sunset.

Sometimes, the hardest fight for life comes in those last moments approaching death. We're just afraid of what comes next.

Lessons for Death

1. Many turnaround consultants don't want to turn your business around.

The reality of the restructuring industry is that many of the people doing the advising either don't know how or don't want to turn a business around. Why? It's too hard and they don't have the experience in actually running a business. Most "restructuring" or "turnaround" advisors are either accountants, bankers, or lawyers. They read numbers and words on a page. They read the *Wall Street Journal* or *Barron's* and they watch CNBC™. They know a lot of technical financial or legal information, but they don't know how to start, grow, manage or lead a company when it's in trouble. They know how to put numbers in boxes. They know how to move numbers around on a page, so they can "restructure" debt. They know how to generate thousands and thousands of words for legal documents. They get paid by the hour. Whether a company is turned or liquidated the hourly rate is the same. In most cases, the only thing that matters is that the debt holders (typically the bank) get their money back (or are reassured that the debt will be serviced). After all, it's the debt holders that sent them to your place of business. If they don't keep them happy, they won't ever see work from them again. For many turnaround consultants, their primary focus is keeping the bank happy. They can't afford to be removed from their referral list. As for "fixing" a company, that's a side note that is occasionally considered "nice." If fixing it brings the bank back its money, then everyone is on board.

Turning a significantly troubled company around requires a tremendous amount of energy, skill at many levels, and luck. You have to marshal all of the employees, all of the suppliers and customers, and all of the assets. You have to keep the creditors and lawyers happy, so they don't shut the business down. You have to get your arms around all of these parties and items, then you need to make everything and everyone better–quickly. That's a lot of work that requires a lot of wisdom and a lot of knowledge about business. So, why would you want that headache when you get paid the same amount of money just to wind the business down—or more, if you file for bankruptcy? Be careful who you hire to help you with your problems.

Task: Interview turnaround consultants. Most likely the bank will give you a list of people they trust. Meet with them but try to find your own credible list to interview. You can start with the Turnaround Management Association for a comprehensive search of restructuring professionals. First, see if you connect with them personally. It's a tough road ahead; you will need both a friend and a taskmaster. A lot will need to be done and a lot may have to change in your company. You need someone who is hardworking; tough but compassionate.

Second, ask them for a list of successful turnaround engagements. Have them show you, line by line, what they did to actually help a client fix their business or improve their situation.

Third, suspend judgement. The tendency is to think you need to hire someone who is an expert in your industry. The reality is that most likely you and your team know more about your industry than anyone you will ever hire. What you need is someone who is (a) an expert in business, (b) an expert at dealing with trouble, (c) optimistic about your chances of survival, and (d) able to help you rebuild trust with your lenders, creditors, suppliers, customers, and employees.

Don't drag your feet too long and don't be too upset at the cost of this phenomena. You are in trouble, the company is drowning, and you need a lifeguard to help you out of this storm as fast as possible.

Lessons for Death

2. If you can't get to a positive cash flow, you have to liquidate in one manner or another—quickly.

At this point, it's about preserving as much value and as many jobs as you can. It's also about repaying your debt obligations as much as possible. If you move quickly and put your ego aside, you can find someone else who can make better use of what you have. Your house is on fire, so you no longer need your furniture...but someone else might. Shed all unnecessary overhead, except the very bare minimum, and then sell off remaining assets quickly.

Task: It's time to amputate. You either cut or everyone goes down with the ship. The biggest mistake that leaders make at this point is that they shave costs rather than cut them deeply. If you are burning cash, you cannot shave your way out of this situation. You need to cut deep and cut fast. Cut major divisions, major customers, and major overhead. It may feel shocking at first, but the company will adjust faster than if you were slowly shaving away. When employees and all stakeholders see "shaving," it will eventually start to feel like they are drowning in quicksand. Cut deep and cut quickly. You will need the additional cash flow to turn the company around.

Lessons for Death

3. Preparing a liquidation analysis is part science, part art.

Trying to estimate the cost of the wind-down of a business and the revenue that might generate is not easy. The goal is to shed as many expenses as quickly as possible while maximizing the liquidation value of all of your assets. Before you begin this process, you need to have a road map (a budget), a strategy, and a team ready to move very quickly. The liquidation analysis should be debated aggressively and should have three scenarios (i.e., worst, most likely, best). You have to be as detailed as possible before starting the process. Get three quotes on all major assets (machinery, real estate, equipment, intellectual property). In a liquidation, the value of an item is not what you paid for it, it's not the value on your books, and it's not the future value—it's the price that the market will pay at that time. How will you know this value? You will know it by the offers that show up. If the offers don't come, you have to lower the price until someone is willing to pay for it.

The irony of some liquidations is that they can actually be more profitable than the previous business model. Why? They strip the company of all unnecessary expenses and present themselves to the public as "Going Out of Business" so their expectations are lowered. In many cases, a skillful liquidator can keep a liquidation going long after all debt obligations are paid off. Have you ever seen a furniture company with a GOB sign on a building for a year or more? They're masters at liquidating. They're making furniture from old inventory, with little overhead, and advertising prices such as 70% off, and they're still making a profit.

Task: Prepare a liquidation analysis—a basic cash flow projection that shows a company stripped of most of its expenses and has an estimate of what will sell and when. It should show a chart that gradually fades to zero, ideally once the debt is repaid or when all assets are collected and sold.

Lessons for Death

4. If you have to sell your business, take the first and fast buck, not the last buck.

When a company is troubled, generally the first purchase offer they receive is the best offer. Why? Because it's losing money. As it continues to decline, the best employees will leave, good customers will start to fall by the wayside, and credit terms from suppliers will tighten up. Pressure will mount on the company from every side. Soon, competitors will move in to completely bury the company. The longer you wait, the less value you will have. If the company is in a negative cash-flow position, generally the sale price will be close to the value of the assets—that's it. Those glory days of closing dinners with investment bankers are gone. Most failed companies that have been around for a long time were once successful, and someone would have purchased them at their peak, but the owner refused to sell because they wanted more. Many of my clients all thought the same thing: "a better offer is out there." There never was. Remember, you don't have the money until there is actual cash sitting in your bank account. Take that first and fast buck and move on with your life.

Task: Make a list of companies or people that may want to buy your company. This may be the most difficult part of the process—putting your ego aside and claiming defeat to your competitors. If you care about all of the people that helped you build the business, you will rise above it and be noble. It may be time to sell to your competitor. Letting them in through the front door to analyze your business and your books may infuriate and crush you, but you may not have another choice.

Your investment banker will concurrently put together a list of other investors. They may be financial or strategic investors who are looking to expand their markets. If you are at this point, you have to run with all suitors.

Caution: Be wary of the overly generous offers at the beginning. LOIs (letters of intent) are just expressions of interest—nothing more. Examine the offers for their "outs." Oftentimes, shrewd investors will put in a high offer to muscle out others at the beginning of the chase. Their goal is to narrow the field so that you are left with few or no choices other than them at the end. At that point they will make "closing adjustments" to the offer. All of a sudden, the value of your business will drop dramatically. Always try to keep as many people in the chase as possible until the very end. Have prospective buyers commit to a "back-out fee"—a fee that they have to pay if they back out of the deal before the sale of the company closes.

Also, incentivize your investment banker to earn more for a higher sale price. Often, investment banking deals have higher percentages on the low bar and they decrease as the price increases. This helps them recoup their time invested in the deal at a lower level and also makes the client feel that they are not being gauged at the higher level. However, I believe it just sets the bar too low. More money and more pay should be the goal for both seller and investment banker.

Lessons for Death

5. Bankruptcy has little to do with you.

If you've struggled with Special Assets and not made significant progress in turning the business around, now your last option to save some jobs and some semblance of your company is to file bankruptcy. You must understand it will no longer be about you. Bankruptcy takes a business process and makes it a legal process. Bankruptcy is about your senior creditors protecting the remaining assets of your company so that they can recoup their loan. Your family, your community, and your storied history only have value if they can make the new owners a profit.

Task: Take some time to get fully educated on the bankruptcy process. At this point, your business will survive without you for a little time. It's in shock mode—it will be frozen for a little while. Take a few days or a week to read everything you can about bankruptcy and speak with bankruptcy attorneys and bankruptcy financial advisors. Try to learn about the entire process before it begins. Digest it. Prepare for it.

Before you file for bankruptcy, develop a communication plan with your legal and financial advisors. This communication plan should be delivered to all of your stakeholders as soon as you file. They need to know the truth and the plan. Don't leave it up in the air; if you don't control the message, the message will control you. Plan a meeting with all of your important customers and suppliers. Be prepared to show them the DIP (Debtor in Possession) budget, which will show them that there is adequate funding to ensure the business will keep running smoothly throughout the process.

Understand that all of your suppliers and creditors will be very upset. Most, if not all, will be unsecured. If you can reorganize the business or sell it at a premium, they will get their past-due bills paid. The chances of that happening at this stage are very small. Sorry; that's just the factual reality. Less than 5% have this success. So, accept that they will be angry. Let them vent. Your problems became their problems. After the steam has left the room, focus on what remains. The reality is that they still want your business. They don't want your business to fail. If you can't run it, they want someone to run it, so they will continue to work with you or anyone who can help them.

Your customers won't be as angry, but they will be concerned about interrupting their own business. Show them the budget and show them that the products or services are funded for the duration of the business. The vast majority will stay with your company throughout the process. Some may make plans to find new suppliers.

Lessons for Death

6. Be certain all trailing liabilities have been captured in the bankruptcy budget.

Every company has expenses that sometimes show up after a bankruptcy has been completed; for example, health insurance or worker's compensation claims. An illness or injury may happen today, but the bills don't show up for weeks or months. When preparing a budget for a bankruptcy be certain to put in estimates for any trailing expenses that will trickle in after the bankruptcy has ended. If you don't budget for this, employees, who in many cases will lose their jobs, will be stuck with those bills. Health insurance providers or healthcare professionals (doctors, hospitals, etc.) will absolutely hound them for payment.

Task: In preparing the DIP budget, make a list of all healthcare, workers' compensation claims, taxes, customer deposits, and any other possible insurance items that need to be covered. Sometimes, DIP lenders are not concerned about these items because those liabilities do not accrue to them. Their goal is to get their loan repaid. They will support the business only to the extent that it preserves value to repay their loan—and that is fine; they have no obligation to even fund a bankruptcy. They can legally foreclose on all of the assets in the loan agreement and liquidate them. You and your advisors need to create a path to protect as many people as possible. This may mean cutting more expenses to be certain the "vital" expenses are covered during and after the bankruptcy.

Lessons for Death

7. Accept that the process will make lawyers a lot of money.

Depending on the size of the company filing for Chapter 11, the process will be expensive. There will be a pre-approved budget with about a dozen line items of expenses going to professionals (consultants and lawyers) to administer the bankruptcy. You will be very upset to see huge amounts of dollars going to people who really will not improve the value of the company. Your unsecured creditors (generally trade suppliers) will be even more upset because they wish that money would come to pay their bills. The professionals in a bankruptcy are there to protect the existing value and account and monitor the sale of assets and repayment of debts. It's not a feeding frenzy; it's more like trying to split up the carcass in an organized manner amongst people who really don't want to get along. There is only so much money to go around so everyone is fighting to get the most they can. The judge is there to try to make sure it is ostensibly a fair fight. But the judge is someone who is trained in law, not in business, so it might not always be fair from a business perspective.

For example, in bankruptcy the professionals record their time in increments of 10 minutes. Somewhere, somehow, someone thought this would be a good way to control the hours being billed. In reality, it takes everyone a lot longer to record an entire week's worth of work if they are jotting down every 10 minutes of their "value." Best of all, in bankruptcy, professionals are legally permitted to charge for the time it takes to assemble their bill each week. So, they make the process cumbersome, then they let you charge the estate for the time it takes to go through that complexity. Imagine getting paid to fill out your timesheet each week?

Task: Go for a walk, go to church, go have a drink. You can't change the law or the practice so let it all go. It's up to the trustee and the judge to keep everyone fair and honest at this point. The fees for the professionals are all pre-approved by the DIP lenders. If they agree to fund them in advance, it's their money, not yours. If they are excessive, the Unsecured Creditors' Committee will fight as much as they can to get more fees cut so they can have more money to recoup on their outstanding invoices.

Lessons for Death

8. Prepare for intense scrutiny of all of your previous actions.

You've filed for bankruptcy, which means a lot of people aren't getting paid for the goods and services they legitimately sold to you. Additionally, a lot of people are going to lose their jobs. In some cases, customers aren't going to get their products. All of this adds up to a lot of angry, frustrated, and depressed people. What does that mean? They're going to go looking for answers. By law, they have the right to go through all of your business to figure out what went wrong and why they're not getting paid.

The law has also put in place provisions to prevent owners and managers from either directly or indirectly benefiting themselves or others. In bankruptcy, a company that has filed is subject to "preference payment" analysis. Creditors are allowed to go into a company and examine all payments made over the previous year to determine if any of the payments were "preferential"—if they benefited one person over another. If they determine that there were preference payments, they can go to those parties and "claw" them back. Those parties will have to pay them to the estate and then the money will be redistributed to all unsecured creditors. If, in this process, they discover that owners and managers were aggressively dumping assets or paying themselves, family, or friends, the estate could go back further in time to examine preference payments.

Task: Ask your legal and financial advisors for a proper definition of "preference payments." With your CFO, go back through 12 months of payments and try to identify what may be considered a preference. Create that list and then try to establish a defense to that claim. Prepare this with your lawyers and don't discuss it openly. Once created, keep it with your lawyers. The day may never come when preferences are analyzed. Each bankruptcy and each UCC is different. However, being prepared in advance will help you and others from losing those fights down the road.

Lessons for Death

9. One last chance: creating a reorganization plan.

A company has 120 days from the date of filing for Chapter 11 protection to submit a plan to reorganize and pay its creditors. All the creditors that are impaired (that will be paid less than what they are owed) get to vote on whether they will accept your plan. If not, they can submit other plans of their own, which will be evaluated by the creditors and the court.

Task: Ideally, you should have a plan prepared BEFORE you file for Chapter 11. That plan should be the basis for your DIP financing. Having the plan in advance will allow for a streamlined bankruptcy process. A quicker process means less fees consumed by professionals and administration.

Lessons for Death

10. Exit gracefully and honorably.

Don't bathe in self-pity. Finish the job that you started. Every person in your business represents your product or service. The way they look, talk, and act represents your business. Every touch point with your customers, suppliers, or creditors represents your business. You are the leader; lead by example to the very end.

Task: Hold your head up high. Act as if it's the first day on the job. Encourage and help everyone be the best that they can be. You may feel dead but you're actually alive. Life will move on. You want to leave a healthy, positive legacy and trail wind.

REBIRTH

After a crisis and a death, there is a tendency to want to crawl into a hole. It's a natural instinct to want to bury and shelter yourself from further pain. Sometimes, it's just too much to handle. You're done discussing the problems of the past. You're done arguing. You are filled with bitterness, resentment, disappointment, and even shock. Everything has changed; dreams and plans have been washed away. Material things are gone. People are gone. Maybe it's all gone. The job, the business, your home, your friends, your money—gone. Your life has changed dramatically and now instead of facing the problems of a sinking ship, you have to take on the challenges of being in a new world. You have to start over but you can't even find the strength to take the first step.

In my case, as a crisis manager and corporate forensic, my entire professional life was surrounded by crisis and death. By 2012, after 20 years in business and working with almost 200 clients, my entire personal existence at that point felt like a black hole. I certainly wanted to be left alone. Any sense of peace and harmony that I had in me years earlier had disappeared. I was no longer that fresh faced kid that was just looking to be "great." I had fought so long and so hard for so many people I was exhausted and was unsure of where I was going. It's easy to get numb and rattled when you live constantly on the front lines of a battlefield.

I spent so many hours in an office that I rarely saw daylight. If I did, I didn't know what to make of it. I didn't have a hobby and I no longer played any sports. I was a stranger to my friends and family. My parents, my sister, cousins all worried and wondered what had happened to me. I had changed once again. I would interact and socialize with them, but my life was completely alien to them. Sometimes they would be entertained by a dramatic story, but most often they would be depressed by it. They would either walk away from me or eagerly change the subject. The stories were just too intense for them. For me, they had become commonplace.

After decades of being immersed in confusion and loss, I seemed to have become numb and more sensitive at the same time. I was paid to process information—thousands and thousands of data points. Every day, I was immersed in analyzing numbers, products, and people and all day long I looked for errors, flaws, patterns, and opportunities. Processing, processing, processing. As problems arose and grenades and bombs went off around me, I stayed focused on the mission—to save jobs, pay off creditors, and save communities. The more I did this the calmer I became. My focus was unshakeable.

Yet, at the same time, I became more sensitive to the smallest of detail. I noticed when a waiter put a fork on a table incorrectly. I noticed when a thread would easily come apart from a shirt. I noticed every item in every room I walked into. Appliances, furniture, decorations, carpeting. I thought about how they were made, how they were sold, their quality. I just kept thinking and thinking. I couldn't stop processing. I evaluated the good and the bad in everything.

When something was bad, I became very angry. To me, it was a sign of deeper troubles and possible, eventual death. When something was good, I was very happy. I celebrated synchronicity and certain corporate survival.

My entire way of looking at the world was put into three buckets: it's bad, it's okay, it's good. All of my responses would then be to not do that, to improve this, or to do more of that.

From my first cup of coffee to my last drink of the day, I was processing the entire world around me. I was no longer a soul; I was a well-honed assessor of life and death. All the lessons I had learned from losing my vision, studying nature, and living among nomads and monks were still inside of me, but I had no joy. I had all of the notes to the music but they were all stuck in my head. I had lost the easy flow of life somewhere in my race to the sun. It had burned up and I didn't know if I would find it again.

Of course, my mind probably could have continued in this manner for a long time. It was trained, and it had already survived through hundreds of horrible phenomena. But my physical body was something entirely different; my body was mangled and broken. I didn't know it at the time but so was my soul. I had just lived through too much pain. Physically and spiritually, I barely recognized love. I knew that, according to the Benedictines, this path on Earth was supposed to be between "me and God alone," but I think I abandoned him somewhere. I respected life, but I forgot how to live. I wasn't prepared to die so it was definitely time to find a new way, again. It was time to heal and start over.

I would have to change my thinking and my habits. I had to go back to my youth, where I spent most of my time learning from my family. They had changed in their lives too, but they were still farmers at heart. From early childhood, I had my hands in soil tending to plants, fruits, and vegetables. We bought very few food items from a conventional store. We grew it, saved it, and cooked it. Living in this manner taught me humility for growing living things. You can't cut corners when you try to grow a life. It requires patience, discipline and consistent effort to bring the best out of a seed or young life. It also requires joy. It requires being light in your skin and celebrating what is brought before you. You learn to enjoy nature as it is presented to you. You can't stand over a tomato plant and yell, "Hurry up and grow. I'm hungry." You plant it in good soil, water it, and pray that sunshine, air, and alchemy do their dance.

I decided to start with small things. Just being mindful of the food I was eating. Being grateful for clean air and sunshine. I started smiling at strangers. I also started taking long walks and enjoying whatever I could see; plants, flowers, insects…and, of course, random dogs and cats. I reminded myself that if I couldn't find joy and happiness in the smallest of things, I certainly wouldn't find it anywhere else. After only a few days, I already found myself happier but I still had responsibilities to address. I had to meet with doctors to deal with some pressing health issues.

A week after my unceremonious firing from my last client, I went for a full body scan. My doctors wanted a closer look at my organs since my lab work showed me to be in terrible health.

Twenty minutes after the scan was run, I sat in front of the cardiologist, looking at a scan of my heart. I noticed a long, thick white line crossing my heart diagonally. I asked the cardiologist, "What is that?"

Plainly, he replied, "That's calcification."

I nodded. I wasn't sure what to make of it. But his next few sentences were very clear to me.

"Domenic, your calcification levels are very high for your age. Currently, you are in the 97th percentile. You are in the top 3% to experience a major coronary event in the next couple of years."

And there it was, poetry, in an otherwise stark and brutal life. My heart was cut in two as I still reeled about the last betrayal and eventually about all of the betrayals. I had set out on a simple journey; to make money and be free. But then I decided to fight for those who were in losing situations. The greater the adversity, the more I was committed to helping all of those involved. But it was hard and dirty work. Now, after spending more than 20 years living in the sewer of the business world, this was my grand retirement gift—a certain heart attack before the age of 50. I had no one to blame but myself. I had chosen the path. I knew the risks…and I did it anyhow. I didn't regret my path; I just wished I would have taken better care of myself.

It was at that point that I thought about that *"jealous mistress,"* the practice of law. I thought about what would have happened if that bloated buffoon, on that first day of law school, had said, "The law is a loving wife. She will embrace and encourage you. She will inspire you to great heights. She will help you bring family and communities together for peace and prosperity." I thought that if he would have said something like that, I might never have gone to Moscow. I might never had become a businessman. I might have been a clerk at the Supreme Court of Canada. I could have built up a career as a lawyer, immersed in intellectual discourse and adjudication. I could have worked in quiet, safe places. I might have studied languages and maybe learned to fly-fish.

I would have eaten three smart meals a day and gone to bed by10 p.m. If only he hadn't told me that the law was a whore, I might have had a simpler life.

But that wasn't the case. My life was not that simple and there would be no easy answers for the years of running hard in dark and dangerous places. I just had to deal with whatever was in front of me at this moment.

I thanked the cardiologist and then decided that if I was going to check out of life permanently, I was doing it in style.

Two weeks later, I was in the South of France, enjoying a glass of wine. I would spend the next couple of weeks just re-learning to savor life and to take my time and just be. As it turned out, it wasn't so easy to do. My body was enjoying the change of pace, but my mind still had a hard time turning off.

So, just like a good farmer, I kept at it. I knew I would have to continue taking steps forward in life and being grateful for all the things that surrounded me.

First step, permanently tie myself to one of my doctors. I married the beautiful and effervescent Dr. Nirvana. She would be my guide on this new path. She is a holistic doctor who truly enjoys the mysteries of life. Patiently, she taught me how to open up my heart and have fun again. To return to my younger years when I dreamed and was full of color and inspiration. To do that, I needed to go explore.

In the next couple of years, I used up all of the few million airline and hotel points I had accumulated when I was working as my wife and I travelled around the world on a whim. It was a simple mission: to enjoy ourselves.

As time passed, I became happier and healthier. I stopped acting like a robot and a field marshal. Everything was moving in the right direction. However, there was still one outstanding problem. It was also my biggest physical challenge: my eyes. My vision continued to deteriorate. I was at the point where I could no longer adequately function through a day. I hung on without having surgery as long as possible but now something absolutely had to be done. I just had to have faith that it would be for the best.

As an eternal optimist, I learned to believe in miracles. But it is still alarming when an actual miracle happens to you. It had been 12 long years of living with extremely blurry, limited vision and incessant pain in my face. But now, my vision was so poor it was time for me to have surgery. I was finally prepared to have two corneal transplants. But then a miracle happened. I found an ophthalmologist who had developed a technique that would avoid having to do an actual transplant. He explained to me that I would need two separate procedures in the bad eye, the left, and one in the other. He told me that he should be able to return most of the vision to both eyes. When I first heard this, I absolutely did not believe him. I had prepared myself for blindness for so long that I couldn't just accept that everything would be better that easily. It was great news but I still needed to think about it.

I went home, had a few drinks, and went to bed. I had the most difficult time with this decision, which really didn't make sense. Either I had these procedures, which still involved surgery, or I have corneas transplanted into my eyes. One way or the other, something had to be done. My real fear wasn't with the surgery; it was with the reality that either procedure might result in total darkness for me.

As it was, I could see color and I could process shapes and images. I could still make out the outlines of life. But, with either surgery, if something went wrong, I could be completely blind. I had spent so much of my life in the shadows, sewers, and hidden closets of the business world that I just didn't want to feel like I would now be living permanently in the dark.

Fear can cripple us more than any actual external force. I had been brave by choice and by circumstance many times in my life prior to this; now was no time to retreat. I had to put down the past and I had to keep moving forward.

I had the surgery a couple days later. I went in, he did his magic, and then he sent me home. The next day I returned, and he removed the bandages. He tested my vision and there it was—a miracle: 80% of my vision had returned! I couldn't believe it. Even to this day, I still have a hard time believing it.

I would spend the next couple of weeks staring at everyone and everything. It had been 12 years since I had seen anything clearly. Unfortunately, I also got a good look at my wrinkles and gray hair. It was such a bizarre phenomenon. My life had moved so fast for so many years in such a maelstrom that it was just a haze. Ironically, so was my vision. Both my life and my vision had been a blurry mess for more than a decade, but now I could see again, and I looked so much older. I questioned where the years went and what I had lived through. I was sincerely overjoyed and humbled to have my clear eyesight restored, but now I had to take a hard look at where I had been in the past 25 years.

It was during this period of time, nearing the age of 48, that I remembered a particularly difficult time in my adolescence. My father was an auto mechanic and he owned a garage. It was a simple two-bay garage with a couple of gas pumps. It wasn't much, but it certainly was more than he had when he first immigrated to Canada.

One day, my father was test driving a customer's car

with his partner. His partner drove, and my father sat in the passenger seat. Five minutes into the drive a man ran a stop sign and drove directly into my father's door. As often was the case in those days, he wasn't wearing a seatbelt. When the car hit him, he put his head squarely through the windshield. He experienced significant damage to his neck, shoulders, and back. He was in so much pain that he couldn't work. Months passed. He went to physical therapy but still had difficulty lifting his arms or walking. Like many small business owners, when you don't work, there's no paycheck. He was able to receive some unemployment benefit, but it wasn't much. There was still the hope that there would be a substantial legal settlement to cover the loss and pain and suffering. He met with his lawyers and they informed him that the best he could expect was an offer that would cover his medical bills. The offer wouldn't even cover his lost wages. No good reason was offered as to why a bigger settlement wasn't possible. They just told him "that's the best we can do."

My father was in tremendous physical pain but now it was nearing six months since he had been at work. His partner did his best to keep the ship afloat, but customers had dwindled. Without two people working full-time, they would lose the garage to the bank. I was 13 when this happened. I remembered the long days and nights of my father laying on the floor, in searing pain, and the worry on my mother's face. We didn't know if he would ever get better. Would we lose the garage? Would we lose our home? What would we do?

Out of options, with no prospect of financial or legal relief, my father woke up one morning, got dressed, and went to work. He worked through the physical pain all day, every day. He hobbled, ached and winced in pain as he maneuvered around and under cars. He worked on cold cement surrounded by grease and toxic fumes. He took his resentment and disappointment in the legal system and put it behind him. He went to work to take care of his family. For me, it was a different experience. I had a great deal of contempt for the lawyers. They should have done more. I felt that everyone should have done more to help him and us. It was then that I was determined to learn about the law.

Now, 35 years later, however, I was realizing that perhaps I had spent my entire adult life reliving that moment—reliving the car accident, physical pain, betrayal from executives, the frustration and fear of further loss and, ultimately, picking yourself up again to provide for your family. I fought over and over for thousands of people who didn't know my name. I fought lawyers, bankers, big corporations, and corporate executives. I fought to keep people from being ripped off and swindled and from losing their jobs and homes. I fought to show people that someone cared and together we could overcome the worst of adversity. I may have done all of this as one continual loop; constantly recreating that moment in time in my adolescence when my family faced the fear of losing everything. It was either a grand coincidence or it was me subconsciously fighting the fight I couldn't when I was a kid.

My entire journey of seeking to learn the best business and legal practices, to learn every aspect of managing people and situations, Russia, China, Harvard, Outer Mongolia, and the Abbey of Gethsemane, half blind and hobbled, might have been my grand journey to learn the skills and to show people that there was a better way to deal with adversity. It may have been my dream as an adolescent to teach others that when faced with trouble you don't need to resort to greed and fear. You don't need to take from others only to benefit yourself. You don't need to lie, cheat, steal, bully, or threaten to kill just so you can have your way. You don't have to assert your power as a hammer or a saw just because you can. My path may have just been to learn and share the lessons from the extremes, from the dead and dying and to show others that there is an easier, less destructive way. It's not just business; it's personal. It's all of us. We are all united by the fact that a business is alive. Kill a business and you kill all of us—if not in body, then certainly in spirit.

After all of the musings and reflection, I finally put down the past and decided to go to a place where I would be forced to learn new things. Where I had to pay attention but I would also dream and create. The one area in which I had rarely spent any time with was emerging technologies. I knew a great deal about business but very little about new tech.

Without hesitation, I threw myself into a world of strangers who spoke an entirely different language than I did. I learned about incubators, accelerators, and angel investors—bright young people with fascinating ideas and surrounded by lines of private equity firms eagerly throwing money at them. It was all about potential; all about the future. Every set of projections went up. It was a world of positive disruption. It was shiny, new, and fresh. This was a world I could get used to. The hardest part for me was trying to be optimistic about the new ideas while remembering all of the things I had learned about failed companies. Every day I was excited about a new potential idea or investment, but by nighttime, I had made a list of all possible threats and weaknesses. It was a constant debate within me. But it was fun.

Then one day, while organizing old books to be put into storage, I came across my old journals.

In the early '90s, I started keeping a journal. It was not a traditional journal of my day's events; rather, it was a journal of lessons and thoughts that I had experienced. Every time I went through something significant in business or life, I would write myself a note. My intent was to write it down and reread it often, so I would be better prepared in the future. I had not written in these journals for many years. But now, as I read them, I thought that I should put them all together in a uniformed binder. Perhaps I could share them with family and friends. They always had questions about business and sought my advice. This could be a pocketbook of some of my best business insights readily available to them. I thought that this was the perfect way to start a new life—take the best from the past and share it with others.

As I started to write I realized a simple but powerful lesson that was important to know for rebirth, for each time you fell and had to start over. It was this: *the more you live, the more mistakes you will make.*

The more you move, the more people you meet, the more you travel, just increases the odds for encountering uncertainty and making mistakes. If you want to live like a painting, frozen in time, then that's the life you will have; you will be mostly preserved, aging slowly without experiencing anything new. However, if you live at full-speed, leaping from one world into another, be prepared for a lot of bumps, bruises, and heartache—but also for a lot of learning, growing, and sharing.

The more I reflected on this concept of balancing living and making mistakes the more I realized that this was a helpful concept to young and new companies and for those that were starting over. That they needed to know this before life and business picked up pace again. I realized that the very same notion that applied to a person was true in a business. A business doesn't fail when it's moving slow. It fails when they move too fast. Most mistakes made by a company are made during good economic times. They are made when it is growing quickly.

Oftentimes, the biggest mistakes are made when a company is at its best. When revenue is soaring, when margins are high, when everyone gets a bonus and the holiday parties are fun—that's precisely when the mistakes are made.

The same thing happens to many of us in our personal lives. When we feel healthy and wealthy is the exact moment when we say: *Sure, I'll have another piece of cake; I'll have another glass of wine; let's go on vacation, let's upgrade—live a little.* And, we take that attitude and feeling into our business. When times are good, we pay a little less attention to the details. We don't focus as closely on customers, suppliers, spending, or employees as we should. Revenue is coming in, all seems well, so we tend to let down our guard. We expand into new offices and new markets. We borrow more money. We invest in new operating systems and hire new employees. Revenue continues to climb, life moves faster and faster. Onward and upward. Then one day, it starts to slow. A month passes and it's still slow. Then two, three, six, and eight months pass. Now cracks in the business start to show.

The new manager you hired wasn't as experienced as you thought. The new operating system still isn't operating properly. You underestimated how difficult it would be to expand into a new market. The rent on your new office is too high. And, the interest on your debt is growing. You try to be optimistic but you can't help ask yourself, "What happened?"

Life happened.

If you're going to live, you're going to make mistakes. If you're going to own or run a business, you're probably going to make even more mistakes. And, the faster you move, the more you're going to miss—misplace, misunderstand, miscalculate.

What can you do about it?

Go back to Chapter 1. Start there.

Move with caution, knowledge, and optimism. Know that you are not alone.

Let me share with you the story of another client, a team of investors that were the brightest of finance and business minds, and how they made mistakes by growing too fast, with too much money.

I sat on a couch listening to Tom, the chairman of the board of a large, multinational truck parts manufacturer, explain to me why the two previous consulting firms had been fired in the preceding months. He explained to me that despite the fact that his company was losing market share dramatically and burning cash, they could in no uncertain terms file for bankruptcy. Apparently, these two well-respected firms had both recommended filing for Chapter 11. At that point, they were fired by the CEO. I said to Tom, "If you hire me, I may come to the same conclusion. And I will be fired too. So, what's the point? Let's skip all of the drama. I don't want the job."

Tom was visibly upset. He said that he, along with the other board members and the principal owners, were very prominent people in the community. They were highly respected financial advisors and lawyers. If they filed for bankruptcy, they would lose tremendous credibility, not to mention that they would be embarrassed in their social circles. So, I told Tom, "I understand. If that's the situation, then why don't you just pay all of your bills? Just pay all of your suppliers and fix the company." Tom became flustered and confused but his answer was very clear. "Oh no. We can't do that. We've already invested too much money into this company." Ahh, I see; he wanted to be respected but he didn't want to act respectfully. Got it. He didn't want to pay his suppliers but somehow he wanted to keep his company alive. Very interesting challenge.

At one time, this was a high-flying company, surrounded by many corporate and finance people who believed in vertical integration. They bought many companies, thinking they would generate "synergies" and economies of scale. Like many strategies that involve multiple acquisitions, they got it wrong. They typically underestimate how difficult it is to incorporate different cultures, different operating systems, and different processes. They also improperly assess senior managers for the roles of a growing company. A good manager of a small company or one division is not necessarily a good manager for a large company. The volume of information and people along the communication channel change. Some people can never adapt to the new environment. In the end, they spent too much money, went into too many different directions, and hired the wrong people to manage all of it. Now, with the lights fading, there was a group of rich guys trying to find a face-saving way out of this mess without putting up any more money.

Despite my reservations about their intentions, I saw this as a unique challenge. I thought maybe there is a way to look at this complex problem and find a way out of it that doesn't involve filing for bankruptcy. I had one condition: that I be employed by the chairman of the board, Tom, and not the CEO. I didn't want the same fate as the previous two consulting firms. I wanted full authority and access to find answers before I could be fired.

The next part of the challenge was with the senior lender to the company. The bank had much more collateral than what remained on the outstanding loan. The bank was smart and kept a close eye on this company. They had brought down the loan over the previous year to a manageable amount. Now, the company was falling apart quickly and was in default of the loan. At this point, they could foreclose on the assets, sell them and successfully collect 100% of the outstanding loan. From a banking perspective, that was the safe play. They were in a happy place when I phoned them to tell them I had been retained by the company. They laughed and told me that I would be fired in two weeks and that they were planning to foreclose in the coming week. I explained my contract and how I was insulated from being fired. I then asked them for a little bit of time to assess the situation. They agreed to two weeks. After that, game over: they would foreclose and 1,100 people would be terminated immediately.

My team and I assessed the four remaining divisions of this failed roll-up. We concluded that three were on life support, but one was stable and could be made very successful. The bank was owed $22M and the suppliers were owed $9M. We decided that we should immediately close three of the divisions. Concurrently, we would transfer some existing production work from the divisions we would close to the fourth location. We then would tighten the process at that remaining division and put new efforts in sales to build that business. In a typical business situation this would not be too complicated. It's common. However, in this situation, with no additional capital, burning cash, and a restless banker, it would be very difficult. And, at the owners' request, we had to do all of this outside of bankruptcy.

This was one situation where it might have been easier to execute within a bankruptcy process. Why? Because bankruptcy freezes all litigation and old debt. It allows you time to implement reorganization plans such as this one. The problem was that Tom and his cronies couldn't handle the public embarrassment, so we came up with a plan to accommodate all of these pressing issues. Essentially, we would move as fast as possible...and beg, negotiate, and pray for a little luck. It wasn't genius but it didn't have to be. Sometimes when you are fighting off corporate death, you just have to be fast to get things done.

We presented the plan to the board of directors. In the plan, we showed a very fast, orderly wind-down of the business that included a systemic pay-down of the bank loan each week. We knew that we had to give the bank a reason to stay in this deal and assure them that the value of their assets would not decline in the process. Paying down the loan each and every week would let them reduce their risk systemically.

At the same time, we would have to transition out of customers, build products for them, collect receivables, keep some people employed, and find a way to pay suppliers without paying the old debt. And while doing all of this, we would also be selling anything and everything fast. We would do all of this simultaneously and pray we wouldn't be pushed into bankruptcy by angry suppliers.

As a matter of law, three trade creditors can petition the court to have a company put into Chapter 11, to protect the assets and repay their debt. In short, we had to shred the business and keep it alive at the same time...with no additional capital and a credit facility that would shrink each week.

We knew this was very risky, but it was the best we could come up with given the parameters of the project. We developed a list of 15 items that could derail these efforts at any time. We wanted the board to know that saving the company was possible, but that these risks, these 15 items, were very real and could result in a bankruptcy filing at any time during the wind-down.

However, if successful, and we pulled all of these things together, we believed that the one remaining division could repay all of the trade debt and eventually return the owners to profitability. They had originally invested $30M and they had $30M of accrued interest. At this point in time, facing imminent bankruptcy, and an ever-deteriorating company, their investment was worthless. We presented them projections that showed that within five years, they would likely get all of their investment and interest returned and possibly more. They were not fictitious or fancy projections; they were conservative and very attainable.

At this point, Tom and the board laughed hysterically. They did not believe any of this could be accomplished in a matter of a couple months. And, they really didn't believe that they would ever get back their original investment, let alone the accrued interest.

They laughed so long and so loud that I figured, "Okay, we're done." We didn't need to sit there and be mocked by these condescending fools.

I packed up my presentation materials, motioned to my team, and we got up and headed for the exit. By the time I reached the door, Tom ran to me. He asked, "Where are you going?" I simply said, "Hey, that's the best we have. Good luck with bankruptcy." He then pleaded with me to stay. I replied, "Try the plan. You have nothing to lose; you're already considered dead by everyone, including yourself." He agreed.

I then added one more stipulation. "I want the keys and the checkbook for six months while I implement the plan. When it's done, you'll get them back. In the meantime, I want the CEO and the CFO (who had created most of this mess) out of my way. We have no room for error." He agreed. I then told him, "Now I need to convince the bank not to close us down tomorrow. They are the first hurdle. If they don't agree, we're dead in the water."

I presented to the bank the next day. They too laughed, but this time I couldn't walk out of the room. If I left they would have issued a foreclosure statement before my elevator reached the lobby. So, I struck a deal with them. I told them, "If we miss our wind-down payment one week, just one time, you can foreclose on us the very next day." This was tremendous pressure but it's what we had to do to have a chance. The bank thought that we were crazy and never believed we could reach the pay-down numbers each week. They thought all of this would blow up quickly so they gave me a chance to try. They basically took a leap of faith because I had worked with them in the past. But, they still needed assurances. They put the pay-down stipulation into the forbearance agreement and included our 13-week cash flow projections. And then the clock started; we had seven days until the next pay-down of the loan.

Next hurdle: the top suppliers that were owed millions. I needed to convince them to keep selling us product during the wind-down without being able to pay them on the existing debt. I walked into the first meeting without a pen or piece of paper. The room was filled with seven executives—the CEO, CFO, COO, and a couple of salesmen. The CEO looked at me and said, "Domenic, I'm sure glad that you are here today. We are eager to see the plan that you have to repay our $2M." I responded somberly with, "I'm sorry. I don't have a plan to repay you. We're going to try to wind the company down, pay off the senior lender, and reorganize under one division. Once we are at that point, then I can develop a plan to repay your debt. At this moment, I don't know what that will be. It may be 10 cents on the dollar, maybe 30 cents. I just don't know."

At this point, the CFO jumped from his seat, furious, and threatened to push us into bankruptcy. I responded by saying, "You certainly can do that but that would only be bad for you. In a bankruptcy process, me and my team will get paid as well as many lawyers and many other administrative people. However, if we file for bankruptcy, I am certain that you and other suppliers will get zero. The company is insolvent today. But, if you work with me, maybe, just maybe I can get you more than zero. I don't know but we should give it a try, together."

They were frustrated, angry, and disappointed. This debt was putting tremendous pressure on their company. But they decided to give me a chance.

I would deliver the same speech to dozens of other vendors. I explained to each one that we could not pay our existing debt but we would be able to pay for parts as we needed them, Cash on delivery, through the wind-down.

Typically, a vendor won't ship any parts if you don't even attempt to pay down the old debt. And they certainly won't ship you product on credit when they know you are winding down. But in this case, we were able to convince them to trust us. One by one, they agreed.

In total, there were 400 vendors that we could not pay. I had my team members on the phone, talking with them every day. We absorbed all of their yelling, threats from their lawyers, and a lot of crying—many of their own businesses were on the verge of bankruptcy as well. They needed every last dollar they could get.

As we managed the vendors, we also sold off assets. Everything that we could see, we sold—fast. We moved quickly but also had to play tough with some of our customers that didn't want to pay their bills. They were waiting for us to file bankruptcy, figuring they could make a few invoices disappear. But, just as we had done with our suppliers, we negotiated and pleaded with them. In some cases, we also suggested that they may not find their tools to make their parts at another supplier if they didn't pay our invoices in full. Sometimes things get lost in a crazy environment. We convinced them that paying us was much easier than playing "hide and go seek." They got the message.

We did all of this for six months. We never missed a payment to the bank, and the loan was completely repaid. The lousy parts of the business were successfully liquidated while we protected the one good division. We were now confident that with all of the noise and chaos removed, that the one remaining division would thrive.

We then secured a new lender for a credit line for the remaining division. Once that was in place, we developed a repayment plan for all of the trade creditors that had stuck it out with us. This plan showed a 60% repayment over the next five years. It wasn't great, but it was much better than zero.

The company continued to improve and thrive as we had planned. Within five years, they had exceeded the projections significantly so they were actually able to pay 100% of their pre-existing debt to all of the suppliers. An incredible outcome no one had expected.

As for the owners, Tom and his cronies, the value of the company also improved significantly. They were now in a position to sell the company and recoup all of their original investment, plus accrued interest, plus an additional profit.

No one laughed at those numbers.

It was a perfect turnaround of a business and proof positive that recovery and rebirth from crisis is always possible.

Lessons for Rebirth

1. Forget the past and embrace where you are today.

One of the most difficult lessons in business is letting go of things that we feel are important to us. Oftentimes it's just the notion of prior success that we are holding on to. You were thriving, you had more friends, people were happier, and everyone wanted to be a part of your world. Now it's gone and it's time to start over. The past will never return. You've changed, and the world has changed. Embrace where you are and build a new success; a new world.

Task: You're starting over. You've made mistakes. You've lived and faced adversity, crisis, and death. Write down what you've learned. Then write down what is next for you, what you want to (i) be and (ii) do.

Lessons for Rebirth

2. Always start with what you know.

Make the exploration about what you know. You don't have to travel far to find something new. Entrepreneurs like to explore. Exploration is great; just understand that the life of an explorer can be exciting but that it is often filled with tremendous challenges. If it's in your heart to find a new planet and new universe after you've closed up one company, then go with God; no one will stop you. Have the time of your life while hopefully learning from your past.

Task: If you are a practical person who thinks the ordinary challenge of business is enough, make a list of the things that you are great at and a list of things that you would love to do. Ask yourself, "How will I do things differently now?" Getting support, financial backing, employees, and customers will be easier if you're an expert in a field and you have a clear plan on how you will be better this time. Don't hide from your past. Admit the mistakes and the lessons learned.

Lessons for Rebirth

3. Decide who you will serve.

When deciding which customers you want to reach, be clear but be flexible. You don't have to serve all segments of an industry or even be in a high-growth or new industry. Just find an area that (a) you are good at, (b) people need, and (c) you can make a profit. Start there, then the market will tell you all you need to know. Pay attention to where your cash flow and profits are coming from. Put all your energies behind both of them.

Task: Look for niches within bigger industries. Try to find an area where there are fewer competitors but that your product or service will still be in demand.

Lessons for Rebirth

4. Learn how to sow seeds.

The most nutrient-dense item that you will ever find is a seed; any seed. It is the nutritional foundation in the seed that will allow people and companies to grow. Ideas are seeds. Create a forum for people to cultivate and share ideas. When in brainstorming sessions, there must be no judgment. People have to know that they won't be laughed at or mocked for a "crazy" idea. In fact, the rule should be, "There are no bad ideas during a brainstorming session." Then, once complete, you can move to the second phase of cultivating ideas—walking through each idea, discussing how it will be implemented, and performing a typical SWOT analysis.

Task: You're building a new team. Hire people who are different than you. Seek out different skill sets and different backgrounds. You need to have common goals and objectives, but it is very healthy to disagree in the planning stages of any product or company growth. That healthy, respectful tension will produce better ideas and a stronger company.

Have whiteboard sessions that are solely for brainstorming. Try to keep these meetings to a manageable number with no more than 10 people. It should be a small enough group so that people can't hide behind each other. Establish the ground rules: (a) There is no such thing as a bad idea; and

(b) When you leave the room, everyone and the process will be respected (no making jokes or insulting what may have come up in the session). Lastly, fill the room with great food. Food makes people happy. Joy, laughter, and celebration are the keys to these sessions.

Lessons for Rebirth

5. Understand the true power of channeled water.

Employees need to be channeled but they also need to run freely once in that channel. Water is at its most forceful when directed and unobstructed. Give them clear direction and clear goals, and offer assistance if they need it—then get out of the way. Employees are the face of your company to suppliers, customers, and each other. They are watching your products and company every day. How they are treated and guided will determine how much your company will shine.

Task: You've been down the road with employees in the past. Maybe you controlled them too much or maybe you ignored them. Now is the time to implement a balanced approach. You are the leader; you're not their pal or buddy— they need and expect clear direction from you. The best employees expect you to get out of their way. Establish the goals for each employee, then step back. Check in weekly, offer help, then back away.

Lessons for Rebirth

6. Rise with the sun.

Leaders offer the light in any organization. Just like the sun, they are there to help illuminate, guide, and provide warmth. They are not there to conduct surgery and burn. If there is too little light the employees will be living in dusk. If there is too much light they will be squinting and irritable. We want just enough guidance to inspire them to climb mountains and walk long distances. Every day set that intention that you will rise and set as the sun in the entire universe of your business; employees, customers, and suppliers.

Task: Ask yourself what your role will be in this new company. Where can you be utilized to the company's best advantage? Are you more comfortable selling, working with design and manufacturing, working within finance developing financial measurements and controls, or recruiting? Pick an area in which you can use your natural talents and then offer help in that area or design it so that it's your primary responsibility.

Next, lay out the vision for the company. Work with each department to develop the drivers of productivity and profitability. Each week make your rounds to the front lines and shop floors. Renew the vision and the drivers. Listen more than you speak. Be the Light.

Lessons for Rebirth

7. Find the right soil.

Too often we neglect the energy that can and should be created by our actual workspace. All offices, factories, and stores are not created equal. When starting a business, cash needs will determine where we will be located. Often it is just where we can afford. However, as we grow, more thought should be given to creating environments where employees and ideas can flourish.

The work environment will vary depending on the product or service that you offer. Each company must understand what matters most in each department and then design that area accordingly. Creative areas like engineering and marketing need loose and free-thinking bullpens. Finance and legal need more structure. Customer Service should be in a quiet area and completely focused on the customers' needs.

Task: Study the work environment. Ask employees what would help them be more productive and comfortable. Study other environments. Look for ways to make changes to keep making employees and customers happier. It's business; love is money.

Lessons for Rebirth

8. Embrace technology and modernization.

Always be on the search for ways to improve the operation of your business and the delivery of your product or service. Accordingly, budget for new expenditures, whether you spend the money or not. Each week and each month put money aside for the eventual upgrading of your equipment. Make it a line item in your cash-flow projections. This way, when it's time to make the purchase, you won't be struggling to come up with the cash or secure financing.

Despite the need for advancements, remember that there are many companies that hardly change and are very successful. Never lose focus of what is most important to your customer.

Task: Study other industries for innovation. Think outside the box by actually going outside the box.

Lessons for Rebirth

9. Till.

The crop and the soil need to be turned every year. To reach new heights and continually be bountiful you need to have expectations. Evaluate your employees, products, and services. Similarly, leaders should be evaluated by their employees. Everyone should be analyzed. Ideally, this should be done once per quarter; once a year at minimum. Standards should be challenged and raised. Those who don't measure up should be given a chance to rise, but if they can't improve over the next two quarters, they should be replaced.

Task: Conduct quarterly employee reviews. They can be 30 minutes long. It should be a checklist of previously agreed upon goals and objectives. Similarly, they should be able to voice their thoughts on your performance. Don't let issues slide. Be clear with people. Guide them and help them but if they don't eventually measure up, they will bring down others. Great people like to work with other great people. Create this culture by having the courage to terminate those who can't or don't rise to the occasion.

Human Resources should continually be sourcing talent. Don't wait for a job opening. It takes time to find great people who are the right fit. Recruit, interview, and keep their resumes on file if there's nothing available at the moment.

Lessons for Rebirth

10. Prepare for bugs and pests.

You can do everything right, but it is still life. Companies are living entities. They are filled with human beings who are fallible. The worst can surface at any time. Thieves, manipulation, and fraud can and do happen. Be certain to have checkers for the checkers. Try to have two separate people validate important data.

Task: Identify the critical junctures of your business: Point of Sales, Manufacturing, Logistics, Finance, etc. Wherever these "absolute certainty" spots exist, think of ways that you can have a third-party verification system. You can't always trust quality control or auditors, because there will always be human error. Have a checker for the checker.

EPILOGUE

When I was 14 I tried out for the track and field team at school just to try something new and different. It wasn't difficult to make the team because the school was small. Essentially, anyone who showed up was put on the starting lineup. I played other sports like soccer and basketball, but I never took part in any pure running events. I wasn't very fast, and I didn't see the point in running for a very long time, so I found a middle distance: the 800-meter. A race that consisted or running twice around a typical track.

As in other sports, I was used to listening to the coach's instructions. For the 800-meter, the coach's advice was simple: stay with the pack; when you round the third corner of the second lap, break away and sprint to the finish. I thought that it was a strange strategy, but I also had no experience in this area so I should just listen to the coach. Certainly, he had to know what he was doing.

For several weeks I practiced running with two other guys, following the coach's instruction. I would come up to the line, the starting gun would fire, and then, shoulder to shoulder, we muscled back and forth for a lap and three quarters. We plodded along, barely breaking a sweat. Then for about 125 meters we would run at full speed. Though I followed these instructions diligently, I never finished first. In fact, I never finished second either. I was third of three, so I was last—every time.

Every day we practiced, and every day I came in last. I knew I wasn't a superstar, but I knew that I was better than last place.

As time passed, I thought the strategy was just dumb. Go really slow, stay next to the other guys, then run and pray you can beat them at the end. I didn't understand it. I thought it was supposed to be a race. I thought you were supposed to go as fast as you could from the very first second—just like car racing. On your mark, set, GO! The coach's strategy was the opposite, however. It seemed more like, "You can start now...if you want," and then the runners would merely gallop, like friendly horses in a field of grass. All of this rummaged around my head, but I was too young and too inexperienced to question the coach, so I just listened and went along with the pack.

A school was allowed to send only two members to the county track and field competition. I was always in last at practice, so I was designated "alternate." A few days before the county track meet, one of the other guys came down with the flu. The coach tapped me on the shoulder and said, "OK, you're up." It was great news.

I was so excited to go to the big meet that I begged my mother to take me shopping for a brand-new pair of shoes. We ran in cleats provided by the school, but I knew it was important to look the part of a star athlete before and after the race. In my family, new shoes generally only happened at the beginning of a school year. This was springtime, so my "old" shoes were meant to last at least five more months.

Nevertheless, I convinced my mother it was a big occasion since it was a new sport and I had just made the team.

It took less than 10 minutes to pick out new Nikes, shiny and white with a baby blue swoosh on the side. Now I was ready for the track meet.

There were hundreds of people at the event. School buses were lined up all around the park. There were flags, signs, whistles, starting guns, and cheering—a lot of excitement and a lot of distraction. It definitely was difficult to stay focused on what I was there to do.

I was happy to be there, but I was also worried because I had always finished last amongst three guys. Now, I was worried that I might finish last amongst *20* guys, in front of all of those people cheering. I didn't know what to expect.

As it drew closer to race time, I became more nervous. I watched guys from other schools gather around the starting line. Some of them were very tall and very muscular while I was a lanky, skinny kid. More and more runners came around and I was certain that I was going to be crushed in a pack of them. I was strong, but these guys were just *big*. I was convinced that there was no way I could survive next to them. I also knew if they were that big they had to be fast. Just by looking at them, I didn't know if I could even keep up with them. The only experience I'd ever had was running next to two other guys who were about my size and a little bit faster than me.

Soon, the race official called everyone to the starting line. My mind was racing faster than I could ever run. I desperately searched for an answer as to what to do; partly to avoid the shame and humiliation of finishing in last place among 20 people, and partly because the competitor in me understood that this was a competition—that it was only about beating the other guys.

Everyone came to the line. The biggest guys huddled on the inside, closest to the field. I couldn't muscle my way anywhere on the front line—I got stuck in the second row. I was very frustrated. My frustration grew to anger and then I made up mind before the starting gun was fired: "I'm not coming in last."

"Bang!"

I could smell the puff of smoke from the starting gun and then all went silent. I put my head down and ran like a charging bull. I plowed into the thoroughbreds ahead of me. I squeezed in between two of them, pushing my way through, and then started running like a spooked deer. I was pure lightning.

For the first three hundred meters I heard nothing—not even my footsteps. I didn't look back and I didn't look to either side of me. All I saw were the white lines on the track. My arms pumped back and forth as I took the longest strides. I was solely focused on running as fast as I could.

I approached the four hundred-meter mark—the halfway point. I saw friends and strangers jumping up and down and waving their arms. I could see their mouths saying, "Go! Go! Go!" I started to get excited; I knew that no one was in front of me. I knew that I was leading. But, then, out of the big crowd on the sidelines, I spotted something strange. I saw my coach. He wasn't cheering; he was laughing hysterically. I wasn't sure what was happening. All of a sudden, all of the sounds came into my head. I heard the screams and the cheers and I could hear my feet digging into the track. I looked back for the first time and I saw that I was at least a hundred meters ahead of the entire pack. There was no one remotely close to me. I thought, *This is great!* But I also couldn't understand why my coach was laughing so hard. I was very confused, but I just continued to push as hard as I could.

And then it happened.

My body started to get heavy.

I was going into the third turn and I now heard feet behind me. I turned and saw two giants twenty meters away and the pack was twenty meters behind them. I thought, *No problem. One last turn and I'm there, across the finish line.*

My body got heavier and heavier. It was as if someone had poured cement into me. My legs weren't following instructions from my brain.

As I approached the fourth and last turn, the two Clydesdales passed me.

I could see the finish line. I continued to dig and push forward but I couldn't catch the two front-runners. They moved farther and farther away from me. The heavy feeling turned to pain in an instant, and my legs started to burn. Nothing I could do would make me move faster.

I now heard the pack behind me. I could hear their feet pounding and scraping and I was certain that I was doomed. I now understood why my coach was laughing. He knew what I was just coming to learn the hard way; that you can't run a long distance in a full-out sprint.

I could hear the pack approaching and thought this would be an ugly, embarrassing lesson if they passed me. I had gone out on a limb, broken rules, and tried something different, only to come in last place, again. Somehow, at that moment, my legs loosened up a bit—just enough to push that last fifty meters.

I crossed the finish line, alone, in third place.

As I fell to the ground, on the side, in the grass, the remaining pack of runners crossed in unison.

Friends and strangers came over and congratulated me. Third place got me a ribbon. I should have felt great, but I was too young and too immature to hear anything other than the few voices that said, "You're crazy."

My coach, still laughing, led the chorus with, "What were you thinking?" Somehow, my coach led me to believe that if I had run the race his way, I could have won, despite the fact that when I ran his way, I was always in last place. As an adult I understand that he was a moron and a lousy leader, but as an insecure adolescent, the message being driven into my head was: "Just follow the rules and go with the flow." I should have been happier with my outcome but, as is so often the case, there are always critics who are there to rain on our parade.

Sullenly, I grabbed my duffle bag and walked up into the stands, near the top of the stadium, to be by myself, to look at the track and think about how I could have run a better race.

As I sat there staring at the track, a very tall man in a sweat suit came over to me. His jersey showed a logo from the university's track team. He sat down about three feet away from me. A long minute passed and then, without any introduction or small talk, he simply said, "Hey, man." I turned to him and asked, "Me?" He nodded and said, "That was the gutsiest thing I ever saw. Good for you. Keep at it." I smiled and then he got up and walked away. I couldn't believe it. A university track athlete was praising me. He actually liked what I did. It was awesome; I felt redeemed. I thought, *Forget the critics. I know what I am doing. I'm good at this.*

What a great feeling it was. I was now so excited to get home and tell my parents what I had accomplished.

Still wearing my cleats, I opened up my duffle bag to retrieve my running shoes. What did I find? Nothing. They were gone.

As I'd attempted my heroic, lunatic dash on the 800 meters, someone had stolen my brand-new Nikes. While everyone was watching me, no one was watching my bag. I hate thieves.

Now, instead of telling my parents that I had won a ribbon, I would have to explain to them why my new shoes were missing. A fun night would now be a night and maybe several days of consternation over wasted money.

What's the moral of the story?

Sometimes life sucks.

It really does.

It's filled with nonstop nonsense.

And business life? It's worse.

It is a life of never-ending challenges. It's up and down. One minute you are crazy, the next you are an inspiration, and then, in an instant, you are at the bottom again, holding an empty bag.

What have I learned about business from the dead and dying? I learned that being an entrepreneur is not about freedom; it is anything but. Many people start a business because they don't want to answer to anyone. In reality, when you own a business, you answer to everyone. You are accountable to every single person within your sphere of influence around that company; the customers, the suppliers, the creditors, and your employees. If you give up a typical corporate job for the life of an entrepreneur, you are trading one boss for hundreds of them.

The dead and dying have taught me that to run a small business one must be absolutely comfortable with a life of uncertainty.

So, why do it at all? Why work every day for what might amount to very little financial return? Why bother to go up against all of the odds of failing companies? Because sometimes doing nothing is worse. The very idea of creating something new, building a team, and sharing your service or product with the community is exciting. It's a new life force. When done properly, it can build and grow and be part of many different communities. In some instances, it can exist for decades. Just knowing that you can create a living entity that shares your beliefs, values, and ideas with so many different people for so long is very exciting—even exhilarating.

The dead and dying have taught me that we should fight for the vibrancy of life as long as we can. Life is hard but it doesn't mean we have to suffer. And, if we are suffering, it doesn't mean we have to die. There is a vibrancy of life that exists in every person and every business. Look for it and make it resonate throughout your entire community. And, if you need help, call me.

ABOUT THE AUTHOR

As an entrepreneur and operational turnaround expert, **Domenic Aversa** is sought after by both global business leaders and government agencies. He has actively assisted companies in dramatic transition for more than 25 years. His experience with corporate restructurings ranges from crisis management to assisting State Owned Enterprises in China and Russia evolve into a capitalist-based economy.

Domenic has served as an educational speaker and managerial advisor on international business development, recession preparation and insolvency issues for many business and academic institutions. Audiences have included the Harvard Business School and the Sloan School of Management at MIT.